Psyc...
Physica... Disease

Edited by

Allan Ho...
Consultant ... ...
Department of Liaison Psychiatry,
The General Infirmary at Leeds

Richard Mayou FRCP FRCPsych
Clinical Reader in Psychiatry
University Department of Psychiatry,
Warneford Hospital, Oxford

Christopher Mallinson FRCP
Consultant Physician in Medical Communication
The Lewisham Hospital NHS Trust

1995

ROYAL COLLEGE OF PHYSICIANS
ROYAL COLLEGE OF PSYCHIATRISTS

187 324 0929

Royal College of Physicians
11 St Andrews Place, London NW1 4LE
Registered Charity No. 210508

Royal College of Psychiatrists
17 Belgrave Square, London SW1X 8PG
Registered Charity No. 228636

British Library Cataloguing-in-Publication Data
A catalogue record for this book is available from the British Library

ISBN 1 873240 92 9 (UK edition)

ISBN 0 88048 638 4 (American Psychiatric Press)

Typeset by Dan-Set Graphics, Telford, Shropshire
Printed in Great Britain by Cathedral Print Services Ltd, Salisbury

Foreword

This book is a companion to a previous joint publication entitled *Medical symptoms not explained by organic disease.* It accompanies joint working party reports of the two Colleges and, in particular, a new report on *Psychological care of medical patients — recognition on need and service provision.* All these publications are evidence of our interest in the wider aspects of medical care and of the value of continuing and improved working relationships between physicians and psychiatrists.

This book reinforces the physician's central responsibility, together with the clinical team, in assessing and managing patients' psychological and social difficulties. At the same time it discusses the ways in which liaison psychiatrists can best provide specialist services together with more general training, supervision and liaison. The findings have implications for individual clinical practice, but also for the training of both physicians and psychiatrists and for those who plan and fund health care.

We believe that there are many opportunities to improve the quality of care and of outcome for patients, some of which can be accomplished with little in the way of extra resources, or even with overall savings. However, it will remain essential that proposed changes in services and the introduction of new technologies take proper account of traditional standards of good medical practice and the overall quality of outcome for patients.

January 1995

FIONA CALDICOTT
President, Royal College of Psychiatrists
LESLIE TURNBERG
President, Royal College of Physicians

Contributors

Christopher M Bass MA MD FRCPsych *Consultant in Liaison Psychiatry, Department of Psychological Medicine (Barnes Unit), John Radcliffe Hospital, Headington, Oxford OX3 9DU*

Susan Davies BA AHSM *Service Manager for Medicine, The Lewisham Hospital NHS Trust, Lewisham Hospital, Lewisham High Street, London SE13 6LH*

Allan House DM MRCP(UK) MRCPsych *Consultant and Senior Lecturer, Department of Liaison Psychiatry, The General Infirmary at Leeds, Great George Street, Leeds LS1 3EX*

Anthony Howell MB FRCP *Consultant Medical Oncologist, Christie Hospital, Wilmslow Road, Withington, Manchester M20 9BX*

Michael B King MD MRCP(UK) MRCPsych FRCGP *Reader and Honorary Consultant, University Department of Psychiatry, Royal Free Hospital School of Medicine, Pond Street, London NW3 2QG*

Bob Lewin MA MPhil *Consultant Clinical Psychologist, Astley Ainslie Hospital, 133 Grange Loan, Edinburgh EH9 2HL*

Peter Maguire MB FRCPsych *Director and Honorary Consultant Psychiatrist, Cancer Research Campaign Psychological Medicine Group, Christie Hospital, Wilmslow Road, Withington, Manchester M20 9BX*

Christopher Mallinson MB FRCP *134 Harley Street, London W1N 1AH. Consultant Physician in Medical Communication; formerly Consultant Physician and Gastroenterologist and Clinical Director of Medicine, The Lewisham Hospital NHS Trust*

Richard Mayou BM FRCP FRCPsych *Clinical Reader in Psychiatry, University Department of Psychiatry, Warneford Hospital, Oxford OX3 7JX*

Graham P Mulley DM FRCP *Professor of Medicine for the Elderly, St James's University Hospital, Beckett Street, Leeds LS9 7TF*

Eugene S Paykel MD FRCP FRCPsych *Professor of Psychiatry, University of Cambridge Clinical School, Addenbrooke's Hospital, Hills Road, Cambridge CB2 2QQ*

Robert C Peveler DPhil BM MRCPsych *Senior Lecturer and Honorary Consultant in Psychiatry, University Department of Psychiatry, Royal South Hampshire Hospital, Graham Road, Southampton SO9 4PE*

John E Tooke DM FRCP *Professor of Vascular Medicine and Honorary Consultant Physician, Diabetes Research Laboratories, Noy Scott, Postgraduate Medical School, Haldon View Terrace, Exeter EX2 5DW*

Contents

10 Setting up a liaison psychiatry service

Editors' Introduction

Psychiatric disorders are common; particularly among people with physical illness. Although some of them are transient and mild, many are not. They contribute to — and to a considerable extent define — the impaired quality of life which is a part of physical illness.[1] Unfortunately hospital practice (unlike primary care) is so organised that physical and psychiatric disorders are usually treated separately from each other. The medical and nursing staff involved in one area often have little experience of working in the other. This unhealthy split has been widened in most parts of the UK by the establishment of Trusts as a result of which mental and physical health services are usually provided by different organisations.

And yet the costs, personal and financial, of failing to integrate physical and psychological health care are considerable. Recognition of this fact has led the Royal Colleges of Physicians and Psychiatrists to organise two joint conferences. The proceedings of the first — on medical symptoms not explained by organic disease — have already been published.[2] This book reports the proceedings of the second, on psychiatric disorders which occur in association with diagnosed physical disease.

These two books may be read in conjunction with a third document — the report of the joint working party of the two Royal Colleges.[3] Together they outline an important and relatively neglected aspect of health service provision. Increasingly, psychiatrists in the UK have recognised that they have a part to play in medical services,[4] but the main thrust of the argument presented at the conference is that the responsibility is not theirs alone. We hope this book will help to stimulate a continuing dialogue between physicians, psychologists, psychiatrists and managers about the best way to provide psychological care for the doubly disadvantaged patients with physical illness and co-existent psychiatric disorder.

This book is based upon contributions to a one day conference in which speakers were asked to cover major themes in the relationship between physical disorder and psychiatric illness, its clinical significance and management. Presentations have been substantially revised and edited for this book and we have contributed brief editorial introductions to the three sections:

Part 1 — The nature of the problem
Part 2 — From recognition to intervention
Part 3 — Delivering psychiatric care in general hospitals

Individual chapters largely focus on specific examples of major medical conditions or treatments which have been chosen as illustrations of basic themes.

The book is principally concerned with the extent and nature of psychiatric problems associated with physical illness and the ways in which they can best be managed by physicians and psychiatrists. We are especially concerned with simple measures that can be incorporated into routine care with selective specialist referral for those most in need and most likely to benefit. Our conclusions have implications for training both physicians and psychiatrists. We recognise too that there will also be a role for others including specialist nurses, clinical psychologists and volunteers in psychological care. We do not discuss their roles in detail. The editors believe that physicians and psychiatrists have a central medical responsibility for the organisation of better care and for continuing supervision and training.

A O HOUSE
R A MAYOU
C N MALLINSON

References

1. Saraway SH, Strain JJ. Academy of Psychosomatic Medicine. Task Force on psychosocial intervention in the general hospital inpatient setting. *Psychosomatics* 1994; **35:** 227–32
2. Creed F, Mayou R, Hopkins A (eds). *Medical symptoms not explained by organic disease.* London: RCP/RCPsych, 1992
3. Royal College of Physicians and Royal College of Psychiatrists: *Psychological care of medical patients: recognition of need and service provision.* London: RCP/RCPsych, 1995.
4. Benjamin S, House A, Jenkins P (eds). *Liaison psychiatry: defining needs and planning services.* Gaskell: London 1994

Part 1
The nature of the problem

The conference upon which this book is based aimed to outline a practical approach to understanding, identifying and treating the common psychiatric problems which accompany physical disease. Approaches to identifying and understanding such problems in the medical setting are outlined in the first section. The central dilemma is that the range of psychiatric responses is broad, and the abnormal and maladaptive tend to differ from the normal and adaptive in degree only. As a result, there is no simple technical solution to the question of 'case identification', no simple screening test which can be applied to detect those needing treatment. On the other hand, vague appeals to the holistic nature of good medical practice will not do: there *are* specific disorders which need to be distinguished against a background of general psychological need.

The most effective way to resolve this dilemma must reside in developing good clinical practice, which should be informed by a reasonable working knowledge of the psychiatric aspects of physical disease:

- the *common psychiatric problems* which accompany physical illness (affective, behavioural, cognitive);
- the *impact of psychiatric problems* on quality of life, handicap, social and physical function, resource use, and (perhaps) the course of the physical disorder;
- the *main aetiological factors* which account for psychiatric problems, some of which will be disease-related (natural history, disability) and some not (psychological and social vulnerability).

After a *general introduction* to the nature of the relationship between physical disease and psychiatric disorder, a number of specific disorders are discussed to illustrate different aspects. In *young diabetics* the common problems include difficulties with compliance and self esteem as well as mood disorder, the consequences of which may be immediate (eg repeated ketoacidosis). Important factors here include age at onset, and the need for self regulation. *Human immunodeficiency virus and acquired immune deficiency*

1

syndrome (AIDS) are associated with high levels of psychiatric disorder of all sorts: do they influence outcome, and is psychopathology the result of brain involvement, the stress of facing death, or the stigma associated with the disorder? *Stroke* poses problems for identifying the common psychiatric disorders because of communication difficulties. Influences on outcome are especially important in the older patient with multiple pathology where the primary physical disorder is not amenable to treatment. The questions of aetiology raised are similar to those in AIDS.

The presentations are diverse, but the messages are clear: psychiatric problems are common, they emerge out of a process involving the patient and his or her social and medical network, and are signals that the process is not going well. These psychiatric problems can be understood only when psychological and social aspects of the patient's life are integrated with the physical history. The cornerstone of practice must therefore be comprehensive clinical assessment. Identification of specific psychiatric syndromes is important, but a narrow diagnostic approach is insufficient. All the authors argue for a broader definition of psychiatric disorder and an approach to aetiology which recognises the importance of social as well as psychiatric risk factors.

1 | Introduction: the relationship between physical and psychiatric pathology

Richard Mayou
*Clinical Reader in Psychiatry, University Department of
Psychiatry, Warneford Hospital, Oxford*

Most people show remarkable resilience in the face of even the most unpleasant illness, but a sizeable minority suffer distress and other psychological consequences (Table 1). There is considerable individual variation depending not only upon the nature of the illness and its treatment but also on the patient's individual vulnerability and circumstances. Awareness and understanding of the psychologically-determined consequences of physical illness should lead to measures to reduce 'medically unnecessary' problems, with benefits for both the patient and the family, and for the most effective and cost-efficient use of medical resources.

Table 1. Outcomes of physical illness which may be psychologically determined.

- Disturbances of mental state
- Impaired quality of life
- Inappropriate or excessive consultation
- Poor compliance with treatment
- Unnecessarily poor physical outcome
- Effect on family and others

The association between physical illness and psychiatric disorder

Table 2 shows the ways in which psychiatric disorder may be associated with physical illness. First, psychological stress and psychiatric problems are common in the general population; in those who are physically unwell, the psychiatric distress may therefore be independent and concurrent. It must not be assumed that psychiatric disorder amongst medical patients is attributable to physical illness — it may be long-standing or attributable to some other stress such as a recent bereavement — although it is of course likely that such concurrent psychiatric disorder will be exacerbated following physical illness.

Table 2. Nature of the association between psychiatric disorder and physical illness.

---
1. Organic physical disorder (delirium and other cognitive impairment).
2. Emotional disorder as a reaction to the illness and treatment.
3. Emotional symptoms as a manifestation of the illness and treatment.
4. Independent concurrent physical illness and psychiatric disorder.

The second important point is that the psychological response to physical illness is not static, and different psychiatric problems may emerge at different stages of the illness.

This can be illustrated by describing the common sequence of response to an acute major illness. There may be an organic mental state (delirium; formerly frequently known as acute confusion), and in severely threatening conditions a degree of denial of the diagnosis and its implications is common. This process of denial is a complex and varied phenomenon, occasionally neurological but usually psychological. It varies from complete unwillingness to accept the possibility of being ill to consciously putting on a brave face to doctors, family and others. Whilst severe denial may be maladaptive in that it leads to inappropriate behaviour, including unwillingness to accept necessary treatment, it is more often an adaptive way of coping with severe stress. The marked denial often seen in acute illness, such as following diagnosis of cancer or acute myocardial infarction, is often transient but a degree of minimisation may persist.

Anxiety is the most conspicuous reaction to the immediate onset and threat of illness, but depression is common later. With recovery from acute illness, mood improves to normal in most people, but persistent distress can be expected in up to a third of patients. Depression and other distresses may also be persistent in chronic physical illness.

The third point to emphasise is that there is no clear distinction between the mentally well and those with psychiatric disorders. As Figure 1 indicates the distribution of emotional distress is continuous, and the distribution curve is shifted to the right in the physically ill as compared with the general population. Only a proportion of the emotional distress associated with physical illness can be classed as psychiatric disorder (ie satisfying standard criteria for

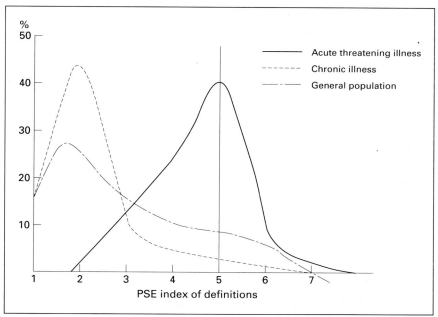

PSE = present state examination — ie research psychiatric interview measuring the levels of psychiatric distress. Level 5 and above indicate diagnosable psychiatric disorder.

Fig 1. *The distribution of emotional distress in the general population and in those with physical illness.*

psychiatric diagnosis and of a severity similar to that seen in psychiatric outpatient clinics); subclinical distress is more common. Only patients with the more severe distress can be classified in terms of standard psychiatric categories, although even here there are sometimes difficulties in applying diagnostic statements to the physically ill. Table 3 lists the commonest diagnostic categories which can be employed.

Table 3. Common psychiatric disorders in the physically ill.

Very common:	Depression General anxiety Delirium
Less common:	Dementia Panic Phobic anxiety Post-traumatic stress disorder Somatoform disorder Mania Schizophrenia-like disorder

Aetiological factors

Factors associated with the development of psychological distress and psychiatric disorder can be classified according to the type of illness, treatment and patient.

It is not surprising that the extent and severity of psychological

Table 4. Factors affecting prevalence of psychiatric disorder in physical illness.

1. Illness factors:	Symptoms
	Threat to life
	Course (acute, relapsing, chronic)
	Duration
	Disability
	Conspicuousness
2. Treatment factors:	Nature
	Side-effects
	Uncertainty of outcome
	Need for self care
3. Patient factors:	Psychological vulnerability
	Social circumstances
	Other stresses (chronic and acute)
	Reactions of others

distress are broadly correlated with the threat and/or severity of a physical disorder. The important components of severity include those listed in Table 4, especially threat to life, disability and duration of illness. Whilst it is possible to make general statements about which physical illnesses are likely to have the most severe psychological consequences, they also have individual significance. For example, rheumatoid arthritis of the hands might have less effect upon a psychiatrist than upon a surgeon or someone whose hobby is intricate needlework. Some drug treatments, major surgery, radiotherapy and other interventions are likely to be particularly distressing. Chronic medical treatment involving the patient in self care may also have a considerable impact.

Personal vulnerability to physical illness varies greatly. In general, those with a history of previous psychological problems, or with a vulnerable disposition or major social difficulties are at much greater risk. However, some people who have previously had difficulty in coping with stress may in fact cope remarkably well with physical illness. Other major life difficulties or acute events may overshadow the significance of their illness. High-risk illnesses, treatments and patients can be identified (see Table 5).

Table 5. Factors associated with a particularly high risk of psychiatric problems.

1. Severe illness:	Unpleasant, threatening, acute, relapsing or progressive illness
2. Unpleasant treatment:	Major surgery Radiotherapy Chemotherapy
3. Vulnerable patients:	History of previous psychiatric problems Current psychiatric disorder Adverse social circumstances Lack of personal and emotional support

Clinical implications of the association

Implications for assessment

Assessment of a patient's psychological and social status is aimed at identifying the common problems experienced by most people with a particular illness, and also the minority of patients who suffer disproportionate and psychologically-determined problems. Table 6 suggests some measures that are useful in this identification. Screening tests may have a role, but by far the most important aspect of assessment is systematic clinical review by a clinician

Table 6. Early recognition of psychiatric disorder.

1. Awareness of the characteristics of the 'at-risk' patient.
2. Systematic review of patients, looking for psychiatric problems.
3. Detection of key symptoms in individuals.
4. Information from relatives.

observant for at-risk patients and key symptoms, who is willing to ask further questions when necessary.

Implications for treatment

Just as assessment is concerned with common problems experienced by the majority and the identification of the extra and special needs of a minority, treatment is concerned both with routine straightforward care and with providing extra help for those who have extra needs. The number of such patients is considerable, and it would be unrealistic to expect specialist services to be able to make more than a small contribution. There is a need to consider:

- how much can be accomplished by the physician and his clinical team;
- to what extent further psychological care can be the responsibility of general practitioners; and
- whether medical and surgical teams need to include people with psychological and psychiatric skills.

Specialist consultation-liaison services staffed by psychiatrists, psychologists and psychiatric nurses have an important role in assessment, in the provision of the most specialist treatment, and in supervision and training. They can work efficiently, however, only if the basic strategy for delivering psychological care to the physically ill has been thought through and implemented.

2 | The young diabetic

Robert C Peveler
*Senior Lecturer and Honorary Consultant in Psychiatry, University
Department of Psychiatry, Royal South Hampshire Hospital,
Southampton*

John E Tooke
*Professor of Vascular Medicine and Honorary Consultant Physician,
Diabetes Research Laboratories, Postgraduate Medical School, Exeter*

> Diabetes is a disease which often shows itself in families in which insanity prevails: whether one disease predisposes in any way to the other or not, or whether they are independent outcomes of a common neurosis, they are certainly found to run side by side, or alternately with one another more often than can be accounted for by accidental coincidence or sequence.[1]

This statement, made in 1899 by Maudsley, demonstrates that psychiatric aspects of diabetes have been known to be important for at least a century. Whilst few psychiatrists today would agree with the sentiments expressed above, there has been a gradual rediscovery of the importance of psychological factors in the outcome of this physical disease. In a condition such as diabetes, characterised by potentially major changes in metabolism with measurable abnormalities of many biochemical and physiological variables, it is perhaps not surprising that until recently clinicians have tended to adopt a 'medical' model in formulating the clinical problems that occur. One illustration of the turning tide is provided by 'brittle diabetes', a problem for which in recent years a variety of physical explanations has been sought. It is now generally accepted that in the majority of cases of young patients presenting with recurrent diabetic ketoacidosis there are considerable underlying psychosocial problems.[2]

Although multiple agencies are now involved in the care of people with diabetes, the most important agent is the person with diabetes, for it is he or she who actively manages the disease on a daily basis (or does not, as the case may be). To accomplish this task (to paraphrase RD Lawrence, the founder of the British Diabetic Association and himself an insulin-dependent diabetic patient), the person with diabetes has to be his or her own doctor, nurse, dietitian and biochemist. It might be added that he or she must also possess (or develop) robust coping mechanisms to deal with a difficult and demanding disease of uncertain prognosis.

Two typical case histories will illustrate:

- the frequency of psychological problems in diabetes;
- the importance of seeking diagnosable psychiatric disorder and also non-diagnosable but clinically important psychological problems;
- the impact of psychological problems on the physical course; and
- the role of the liaison psychiatrist in this context.

Case 1

AB is a young man, now in his early 20s, who works in an office in a financial institution, and who developed insulin-dependent diabetes at the age of 14. There was no previous family history of the condition. His mother died of cancer at the age of 36, and AB grew up with two sisters, a stepsister and stepbrother. Initially following the diagnosis of diabetes AB coped well, but at times his behaviour became rather aggressive and difficult. After leaving school he went abroad for a year to live with an aunt, described as 'someone who stood no nonsense'; in his own estimation this was a year of great success and fulfilment for him.

On his return to the UK, he 'graduated' to the young adult diabetic clinic. There followed a series of admissions to hospitals with hypoglycaemia, often associated with excessive alcohol consumption. Concerns were prevalent at the time about human insulin and hypoglycaemia unawareness, but it soon became clear that this was a red herring in his case. He had a number of attacks of severe hypoglycaemia, culminating in a road traffic accident which occurred whilst he was driving without insurance. He subsequently began a relationship with a married woman who was ten years his senior. During this period, his clinic attendance was infrequent. He was devastated when the relationship broke up nine months later.

AB's frequent attacks of hypoglycaemia continue. It is of note that these occur at home and never at work. He gives an impression of being oblivious to the risks of his condition, and has ignored all the efforts of the diabetes team to support and assist him to deal with this problem.

Discussion

Physicians may often approach a problem of this kind using a narrow 'medical' model, concentrating on the biochemical and pharmacological aspects of the case. There is an equal danger that psychiatrists may be trapped in a narrow 'mental' model and respond to a request for assistance with such patients by screening for 'formal' mental illness — and doing nothing more. This is a necessary part of psychological management, but it may not be sufficient to meet fully the needs of the patient. The psychiatrist working in a liaison setting must do more.

In the case under discussion, the principal diagnosis to consider first would be of a depressive disorder. Agreement on standard criteria, such as those of DSM-IV[3] (Table 1) or ICD-10, for recognition of depressive illness has facilitated this process, and has formed the basis for educational initiatives such as the 'Defeat Depression' campaign of the Royal Colleges of Psychiatrists and of General Practitioners,[4] which could usefully be extended into the general hospital setting. Diagnosis of the syndrome of major depression is clinically useful because it represents a threshold at which treatment with antidepressant medication yields greater benefit than placebo. Some difficulty remains, however, in assessing depressive symptoms in patients with co-existing physical disease. The physical symptoms which form part of the syndrome of major depression (eg weight or appetite change, fatigue or sleep disturbance) may result from the physical disease, and thus be of diminished value in discriminating between patients with

Table 1. DSM-IV criteria for major depression.[3]

Diagnosis of the syndrome of major depression requires the patient to have either of the first two features listed, plus at least four of the remaining seven, for a period of at least two weeks, without any other primary cause:

- Depressed mood
- Loss of interest or pleasure
- Feelings of worthlessness or guilt
- Impaired concentration
- Thoughts of suicide
- Loss of energy and fatigue
- Reduction or increase in appetite or weight
- Insomnia or hypersomnia
- Psychomotor retardation or agitation

and without the syndrome.[5] This issue is of considerable importance in the design of research studies, but in a clinical context
the most practical approach is to use the established syndrome
definition as a basis for an empirical trial of treatment.

As mentioned above, it is important that psychiatrists working
with patients with physical illness do not restrict themselves solely
to consideration of formal mental illness. The principal reason is
that symptoms of lesser severity, which may be considered 'subclinical' in physically healthy patients, may interact in various ways
with physical disease. They may, for instance, affect self care, and
this in turn will affect outcome in a chronic disease such as diabetes. It is therefore important that the liaison psychiatrist extends
the assessment to include a formulation of the case and devises a
management plan, rather than just providing a diagnostic opinion
to the physician.

In the case being considered here, additional factors to appraise
include the apparent interpersonal difficulties experienced by the
patient, possible unresolved grief about the early death of his
mother, and problems with self image and sexuality. It is vital both
to recognise that the patient's self care behaviour may be used to
express feelings that have nothing to do with the diabetes itself
and also to view poor metabolic control as multifactorial, rather
than entering into a sterile debate about whether its origins are
physical or behavioural. An additional difficulty in a case such as
this is arranging the involvement of a mental health professional.
Many patients are reluctant to accept outside referral to a psychiatrist. This process is made much easier and simpler if the mental
health specialist works with the diabetes team in an integrated way.
Unfortunately, this facility is all too rare in Britain at the time of
writing.

Case 2

CD is a woman in her early 30s who works in an administrative
position. She first presented with diabetes at age 12, and gives a
vivid description of the authoritarian approach taken initially to
her condition which she greatly resented. She was referred to an
adult physician in 1981, who remarked that she demonstrated
depressive symptoms and took little interest in her condition,
seldom monitoring her blood or urine glucose levels. She did not
comply with the suggested dietary regime, and was considerably
overweight.

She was transferred to the diabetes service in 1987. She gave an initial impression of 'non-acceptance' of her condition. All contacts with her were confrontational, and she frequently complained about the service — although some of her comments were both perceptive and constructive. She had a particular dislike of dietitians whom she saw as excessively restrictive in their outlook.

She married a man who was twice her age, and her stepson was killed in a road traffic accident shortly afterwards. In 1989 she developed severe neuropathic pain which precluded sleep and enforced a review of her poor metabolic control. She described herself at this time as a 'chocoholic', giving this as one reason why her disease could not be controlled.

The stance taken in the clinic was to accept rather than confront her high intake of sugary foods, and to develop a personalised insulin regime that improved her glycaemic control whilst allowing a relatively free diet. This was followed, interestingly, by a period of loss of confidence during which she became very demanding of the diabetes service — almost as though she was testing its ability to respond to her needs. She subsequently settled well, with much improved standards of metabolic control. She developed proliferative retinopathy in 1990, but this has settled following laser treatment, with visual preservation. She now has a much more constructive relationship with the diabetes service.

Discussion

In this case, one decision facing the liaison psychiatrist is whether or not the patient has an eating disorder requiring specialist treatment. In addition, there has been a lengthy period of angry rejection of the diabetes and its treatment, which has coloured all the patient's relationships with professionals involved in her care. As in the first case, standard diagnostic criteria can be used to address the first question (Table 2). Whilst adolescent and young adult females with diabetes do not appear to be at any greater risk than the non-diabetic population of developing an eating disorder, the prevalence of such conditions in this age group is high (approaching 5%), and these disorders are therefore an important contributory factor to impaired self care.[6,7] Clues which may help the clinician recognise an eating disorder include the age and sex of the patient, the presence of unexplained poor metabolic control, marked weight fluctuation, variation in insulin requirements, and preoccupation with body shape or weight. In addition to patients who meet the full criteria for an eating disorder, there are patients with eating

Table 2. DSM-IV criteria for eating disorders.[3]

Anorexia nervosa
- Body weight 15% or more below healthy weight for age and height
- Intense fear of gaining weight, even though underweight
- Disturbance in the way body weight, shape or size is experienced
- Absence of at least three consecutive menstrual cycles (in females)

Bulimia nervosa
- Recurrent episodes of binge eating (rapid consumption of a large amount of food in a discrete period of time)
- A feeling of loss of control over eating during binges
- Regular self-induced vomiting, use of laxatives or diuretics, strict dieting or fasting, or vigorous exercise to prevent weight gain
- A minimum average of two binge-eating episodes a week for at least three months
- Persistent overconcern with body shape and weight

disorder symptoms of lesser severity. Again, such patients may be viewed as having a 'subclinical' problem if they are physically healthy, but if such symptoms co-occur with a disease such as diabetes their clinical importance is greatly increased. Unfortunately, little research has been conducted to date on the management of such 'subthreshold' or 'partial syndrome' eating disorders.

Attention must also be paid to the relationship between the patient and her medical attendants. There appears to be a continuation of a pattern of behaviour common in adolescence in which there is conflict between the patient expressing dependence on the clinic and asserting her autonomy. The approach taken in this case now appears to have worked satisfactorily, at least for the present. Not all clinicians would have found it easy to adopt such a relaxed approach, and again the assistance of a mental health professional working closely with the diabetes team would have been helpful.

Conclusions

The main points which emerge from this brief analysis are as follows:

1. The psychological status of the person with diabetes is a principal feature, if not *the* principal feature, governing self care and the outcome of the physical disease. It is important that this fact is rediscovered, given the current emphasis on good glycaemic

control that has emerged with the publication of the results of the diabetes control and complications trial from the USA.[8] If good control is to be achieved, both a good understanding of health-related behaviour and appropriate psychological care are paramount.

2. Specific psychiatric disorders are slightly more prevalent overall amongst patients with physical disease, and these require recognition and active management.[9] Two of them, depression and eating disorders, are of particular importance among young adults with diabetes. Milder, 'subclinical' psychological difficulties are of increased clinical significance when they co-occur with diabetes, and they must also be considered because of their impact on self care. This is an important difference between the practice of consultation-liaison psychiatry and general psychiatry.

3. Close liaison between medical services and those offering psychological care is the key to the successful management of these clinical problems. The availability of such close links is currently limited, and psychiatrists and physicians need to be united in pressing for their further development.

References

1. Maudsley H. *The pathology of mind*, 3rd edn. New York: Appleton, 1899
2. Gill GV, Husband DJ, Walford S, Marshall SM, *et al*. Clinical features of brittle diabetes. In: Pickup JC, ed. *Brittle diabetes*. Oxford: Blackwell Scientific Publications, 1985: 29–40
3. American Psychiatric Association. *DSM-IV: diagnostic and statistical manual of mental disorders*. Washington, DC: American Psychiatric Association, 1993
4. Paykel ES, Priest RG. Recognition and management of depression in general practice: a consensus statement. *British Medical Journal* 1992; **305**: 1198–202
5. House A. Mood disorders in the physically ill — problems of definition and measurement. *Journal of Psychosomatic Research* 1988; **32**: 345–53
6. Fairburn CG, Peveler RC, Davies BA, Mann JI, Mayou RA. Eating disorders in young adults with insulin dependent diabetes: a controlled study. *British Medical Journal* 1991; **303**: 17–20
7. Peveler RC, Fairburn CG, Boller I, Dunger D. Eating disorders in adolescents with insulin-dependent diabetes mellitus. *Diabetes Care* 1992; **10**: 1356–60
8. Diabetes Control and Complications Trial Research Group. The effect of intensive treatment of diabetes on the development and progression of long-term complications in insulin-dependent diabetes mellitus. *New England Journal of Medicine* 1993; **329**: 977–86

9. Mayou RA, Peveler RC, Davies B, Mann JI, Fairburn CG. Psychiatric morbidity in young adults with insulin-dependent diabetes mellitus. *Psychological Medicine* 1991; **21**: 639–45

3 | HIV infection and AIDS

Michael B King

Reader and Honorary Consultant, University Department of
Psychiatry, Royal Free Hospital School of Medicine, London

Our knowledge of the psychological aspects of human immuno-deficiency virus (HIV) infection and acquired immune deficiency syndrome (AIDS) continues to evolve. This is a new problem, new treatments are being developed, and the amount of hope that patients can hold continues to change. Thus, it is not a static field but one in which there has been an enormous expansion both of knowledge and of services. This expansion has in fact led to a degree of criticism that so much money has been poured not only into AIDS medical research but also into psychological research and support systems. Nevertheless, many people consider that the models developed for the psychological support of people with HIV infection and AIDS could be applied across other medical and psychological interfaces.

This chapter will cover the following areas:

- how common is psychiatric disorder in HIV infection and AIDS?
- what sort of psychiatric disorders are seen in HIV infection?
- the aetiology of psychiatric disorders, including predictors of psychological distress.

The sorts of psychological difficulties encountered by people with HIV infection will be discussed rather than ways of intervening to help such difficulties.

How common is psychiatric disorder in HIV infection and AIDS?

In the 1980s, when HIV infection was first appearing as a distinct and increasingly prevalent disorder, there was considerable interest in the rate of psychiatric disorder in this population. One difficulty in determining how common psychiatric disorder is in HIV infection is of obtaining representative samples. It is even more difficult to select control groups. Cases need to be defined not just by HIV infection itself but also by the stage of the infection. This is important because emotional disorder may vary depending on the nature or state of the HIV infection.

Early studies suggested that the rate is very high and that most people with HIV infection and AIDS encounter some sort of psychological difficulty. The trouble with these early studies is that they were often based on case series of patients referred to psychiatrists.[1] Although these were important series because they helped to understand the *types* of disorders that occurred, they were not particularly helpful in demonstrating *how common* disorders are in the general population of people with HIV infection. Later studies more firmly based in epidemiological methods revealed that rates of psychological disorder are much lower than previously suggested and comparable with rates in other serious physical disorders.[2]

Other early work involved cross-sectional studies of unselected patients with HIV infection and AIDS. Studies such as these are forced to rely on patients who are attending clinics; it is impossible to do basic house-to-house epidemiological work with this type of disorder. One study, in the late 1980s, assessed unselected patients attending HIV specialist clinics in London.[2] This and other later studies have shown that a recognisable psychiatric disorder that would benefit from some form of intervention is found in about one-third of patients. It should be emphasised that this is within a population who are not seeking help for psychological problems but who have come to an HIV clinic for routine surveillance. Most of the psychological disorders found were depressive or adjustment disorders of mild or moderate severity.

Longitudinal studies of psychiatric disorder[3] have essentially replicated the findings of the cross-sectional studies in terms of how much psychiatric disorder is found, but they have been important in the search for risk factors and protective factors: who gets ill, when and why? (This subject will be discussed further in relation to predictors of psychological distress.)

More recent data have shown that rates of psychiatric problems tend to be higher in women with HIV infection than in similarly affected men. There have not been many studies of women in western countries, however, as the number of women with HIV infection is low. There have been one or two in the USA, one in Italy[4] and one in England.[5] In the last study, women living in France and England were compared in terms of the sorts of services they received and the kinds of psychiatric disorders found amongst them. Up to 50% of the women had psychological problems of a type severe enough for intervention. Perhaps surprisingly, these occurred more commonly in France. The difference between the two countries was difficult to explain, but closer examination of the counselling services offered around the time the women were notified of their infection showed them to be much better developed in England. It is impossible to be certain that preparation of the patient for an HIV antibody test and the quality of post-test counselling are crucial factors in later psychological disorder, but this seemed to be the only factor that could be seen as a predictor of higher rates of disorders in France. It must be added, however, that many of these women belonged to groups that are subject to high rates of psychological disorder. For example, some were drug users, a very small minority were prostitutes, and others were partners of drug users. Although many of these women came from disadvantaged backgrounds, such deprivation exists both in England and France. A factor which may explain why rates of emotional disorder in women are higher than in men is that they may be less good than men at using the services available.

What sort of psychiatric disorders are seen in HIV infection?

It is hardly surprising that *adjustment disorders* and *substance abuse* are by far the commonest disorders encountered. HIV is a life-threatening diagnosis and many people react badly at first. Later, however, most adapt to the news, and rates of disorder are surprisingly low. There was considerable concern in the late 1980s about HIV testing. Knowledge of HIV infection was regarded as depressing and something about which nothing could be done. In some clinics in Britain people were tested without being informed of the results; patients would merely be told to come back on a regular basis. This type of practice was unwarranted and appeared to be based on the inaccurate assumption that people would be unable to adapt to the knowledge that they had HIV infection.

Time has passed, new treatments have been developed and now people are encouraged to be tested. There is considerable evidence from prospective studies in the USA that a person's psychiatric state improves after having a test even if the test is found to be positive.[6] It appears that *uncertainty*, either about whether the individual has HIV infection or about the stage of the infection, is the cause of much emotional distress.

There has also been concern about reports of increased lifetime risk for psychiatric disorders in people who develop HIV infection.[7] It may be that higher rates of lifetime disorders occur in gay men and drug users than in the general population, but the evidence for this is rather poor as it is often based on men who already have HIV infection rather than on HIV-negative gay men and drug users. Many of the studies which have included HIV-negative gay men have based their work on men coming forward for testing who are not necessarily representative of the wider population of gay men.

Depression and suicidal thoughts are common in people with HIV infection. Although depressed mood is most often seen in the context of an adjustment disorder, frank clinical depression can also occur.[2]

It was originally thought that *suicide* rates were not particularly elevated in people with HIV infection, although there was considerable *talk* about suicide among these patients. Many patients say that they will commit suicide when they get ill — they are all right *now*, but when they cannot cope with their illness they will take their life. Later it changes to when they become *more* ill they will commit suicide — and so on. It is now known that the suicide rate in people with HIV infection is elevated compared to other populations. The results of a study carried out in New York in the late 1980s[8] are well known and have been replicated many times. This study found that the suicide rate in people with HIV infection was 30–40 times higher than the rate for men of the same age in the general population. One sobering aspect of this study was that 25% of the people who committed suicide did so by jumping out of a window of the hospital building in which they were being treated. It behoves us to be vigilant about people under our care.

Physicians and other professionals are sometimes faced with requests from their patients for euthanasia. In Holland, where euthanasia has been decriminalised in certain situations, the latest figures show that up to 23% of AIDS patients who request euthanasia actually undergo it.[9] Although this is probably not the place to enter into a detailed discussion of the pros and cons of euthanasia, it is worrying that many patients undergo euthanasia in Holland apparently without a prior careful psychiatric assessment.

There also appears to be some concern about the rate of *personality disorders* in people with HIV infection. Much of the psychiatric liaison with HIV infected patients involves helping those with personality disorders. People with frank, distressing personality disorders, who are very chaotic in their self care, are difficult for physicians to look after. An extra dimension is that many professionals worry about the behaviour and responsibility of personality-disordered patients and the risk of sexual spread of disease; they frequently have to cope with patients who tell them about their sexual exploits, including how much unprotected sex they are having, many of them covertly challenging the doctor to take some action to prevent it.

Finally, the people who have *obsessive compulsive worries* that they might be HIV-positive cause a considerable amount of work for liaison psychiatrists in the area of HIV, but it must be remembered that the professionals who encounter most of these patients are general practitioners. The most useful techniques of intervention in these cases have included a combination of cognitive behavioural therapy with an agreement between the patient and therapist that the latter will not provide repeated reassurance.[10]

Psychotic and organic disorders

Psychotic disorders

Psychotic disorders occur uncommonly in people with HIV infection, are demanding to treat and may be difficult to distinguish from organic states. Patients with dementing illnesses may become obviously deluded and hallucinated, but there seems to be a group of patients who develop a psychosis *de novo*, sometimes without any other signs that they have HIV; in other words, psychosis is the presenting illness. Usually, however, they are known to have HIV and the psychosis develops at a relatively late stage. All the cases seen in the Royal Free Hospital over the last five years — and there have not been many, perhaps about six a year — have been manic in character, with features of overactivity, grandiose delusions and irritability. There is much talk in the literature about a specific HIV psychosis, characterised by manic features. These states are rare and, as far as the present author is aware, only one group has examined their prevalence in the context of a known population denominator with access to the same service. This study reported that manic states in people with HIV infection are four times more common than in the general population.[11]

The difficulty is that these psychotic states often appear abruptly, with the individual sometimes changing from a normal mental state to a highly aroused and completely unmanageable one in 24–48 hours — this is much less common in the mania seen in manic depressive psychosis unrelated to HIV infection. Such patients can cause absolute chaos if they are under treatment on a medical ward and may prove difficult to manage.

Management will not be discussed here in any depth but I want to challenge one assumption about treatment. Many people believe that patients with HIV are particularly sensitive to antipsychotic drugs, particularly to their anticholinergic and parkinsonian effects. In my experience, this is true only when the immune function level is low and patients are physically quite unwell. When people are not particularly physically ill, high doses of antipsychotic drugs may have to be used to gain control of these manic states.

The manic psychoses in HIV infection are of interest because they draw attention to the processes involved in the central nervous system (CNS). They often occur in people who have not previously suffered psychotic illness. When they resolve, patients are almost always left with some cognitive deficit, which is strongly suggestive of an organic aetiology.[11]

Chronic organic states

Chronic organic states affecting the CNS in people with HIV infection have also caused enormous controversy for years. Early CNS changes can be detected in HIV-positive people by EEG or by demonstration of abnormalities in the cerebrospinal fluid. The virus enters the brain at the time of the primary infection, probably via macrophages. Sometimes people suffer a meningitic syndrome when first infected, although this is unusual.

There was much confusion about the extent of cognitive impairment in HIV infection in the mid-1980s because studies in the USA, that were hampered by small numbers and overly sensitive tests, reported that HIV-positive people who were otherwise well had subtle cognitive changes that put them at risk.[12] The armed services in the USA were immediately subjected to screening, and the US Defence Department announced that seropositive military personnel would be removed from sensitive or stressful jobs.[13] This caused great concern in the armed services and was almost certainly not worth doing. Nevertheless, the aviation authorities in the USA still recommend screening their pilots because of this worry about subtle cognitive deficits.

The problem with many studies of cognitive function in HIV infection is that they are not well controlled for past psychiatric history, drug use, IQ, education, and even sleep deprivation (which has an effect on performance on many of the cognitive tests because quite subtle changes are being sought). Another important factor concerns where these tests take place. They are frequently carried out in an HIV clinic. Patients do not sleep well the night before because they are worried about what they might be told about their CD4 count or their physical state, and consequently often perform poorly in the tests. The most important factor, of course, is the salience of the test. Many researchers in the USA and Britain have tried to control for all these factors, sometimes comparing the performance on cognitive tests of young men with neurotic problems with that of HIV-positive men, thereby controlling for psychiatric factors as clearly as possible. It is never possible, however, to control for the salience of the test. A test has a different meaning to someone who is HIV-positive than to an HIV-negative person acting as a control. Almost all people with HIV infection know they have a small chance of acquiring a dementing illness and become nervous and upset about having to do these tests which obviously impairs their performance. There is also a strong link between reporting depressive symptoms and doing poorly on the cognitive tests.[14]

Most well conducted controlled studies have now shown that there are no important cognitive deficits in people who are HIV-positive, physically well and not significantly immuno-compromised,[15-17] although surprising claims have been made that this debate has been affected by researchers with an emotional investment in demonstrating this to be true.[17]

There is no doubt, however, that there is a dementing syndrome which usually occurs when immunosuppression is at levels at which people develop physical illness. This used to be called AIDS-dementia complex, a term that was not particularly useful because it was too broad, and because in some cases the syndrome appeared to be reversible to some degree. The World Health Organisation (WHO) and the American Academy of Neurology (AAN) have come up with new terminologies. The WHO has proposed the term HIV-1 associated cognitive/motor complex (HACC) to incorporate all grades of severity.[18] A possibly more useful division between mild and severe impairment is the AAN's suggestion of dividing HACC into the more severe HIV-1 associated dementia complex and the milder HIV-1 associated minor cognitive/motor disorder.[19]

HIV-associated dementia

The dementia seen in HIV infection has often been considered to be associated with disease affecting primarily subcortical structures of the brain. The clinical picture is one of subcortical dementia with withdrawal, personality change and apathy, in the absence of abnormalities such as dysphasia and apraxia. Recent pathological evidence, however, shows that up to a third of the cortical neurons are lost, particularly in the frontal cortex, even in the absence of clinically significant cognitive impairment.[20] Fully developed HIV-associated dementia will occur in up to one-third of patients but usually only when they become quite ill; it is usually a terminal event.

The aetiology of psychiatric disorder

How can this range of psychiatric problems be put into context? I will briefly discuss a study in which a direct comparison was made between patients with HIV infection and patients with other medical disorders who were referred to liaison psychiatrists.[21] Seventy referrals to the HIV psychiatric liaison service of the Royal Free Hospital in London were matched with 70 referred to the general psychiatric liaison service. Organic, adjustment, mood and personality disorders were the most common referral problems, but there were no particular differences between the two patient populations. Thus, the patients with HIV infection presented with many of the same sorts of emotional problems as patients with other medical disorders. This cannot be emphasised enough: the similarities between people with HIV infection and AIDS and patients with other serious illnesses are much greater than the differences. Interestingly, alcohol abuse was more common among the comparison patients. Many studies have reported that alcohol is a particular problem amongst people with HIV infection, but in the context of the general psychiatric liaison service it is clearly a problem for a significant number of *all* people admitted to hospital. A history of psychiatric problems is also said to be more common among people with HIV infection, but in this study the opposite was true, with such a history occurring more commonly in the comparison group.

Many factors are important in precipitating psychiatric problems in people with HIV infection. There is the obvious stress of suffering a life-threatening disorder, prejudice about HIV infection and sexuality, and uncertainty about the illness.

Life-threatening disorder

The problems relating to the stress of having a life-threatening illness are common to many disorders. In a study recently completed in Sao Paulo, Brazil, in which patients with HIV infection were compared with patients with life-threatening haematological disorders, there were few differences in the rates of psychiatric disorder.[22]

Prejudice

Although prejudice about HIV infection or homosexuality does not appear to be strongly predictive of the development of psychiatric disorder, at least in Western countries,[2] it is an issue of considerable importance to people with HIV infection. Prejudice over sexuality or HIV infection does not mean simply that people feel that others may have negative opinions about them or look at them in a disdainful way, but it involves overt verbal or physical abuse by their family or others. Family members do not always react well to the news that their son or brother is homosexual *and* has HIV infection. Patients experience a considerable amount of guilt and self blame over their sex life, whether heterosexual or homosexual, together with worries that they may have infected others. These are very real issues which are particular to patients with HIV infection and in which counsellors, psychiatrists and psychologists must become involved.

In contrast to reports from the West, the study in Brazil found that prejudice against people with HIV infection was a strong factor in predicting psychiatric problems among them.[22] This must be seen in the context of a country in which there have been reports over many years of considerable public prejudice against people with HIV infection. Furthermore, homosexuals in Brazil appear to be a particularly stigmatised group.[22]

History of psychiatric and personal problems

Past psychiatric and personal problems are strong predictors of the development of a psychiatric disorder at some point during the course of HIV infection — a finding that has been replicated in many studies of psychological factors in HIV infection, as it has in studies of psychiatric disorder associated with other physical illness. This risk factor is often missed in clinical situations when professionals fail to ascertain how patients have coped with previous illnesses or stressful situations. Nevertheless, such histories are not infallible predictors that a patient will become seriously distressed again with the advent of HIV infection. Sometimes people experiencing the most difficult life and social situations grasp on to this illness as something to help them cope, and they adapt to it in a paradoxical way. It seems to represent a challenge in what was previously a meaningless life.

Health worries

Health worries are also an important predictor of psychiatric problems. People who constantly ruminate about their physical health, who report swollen lymph nodes, a cough and so on to their doctors, and in whom no pathology can be found are almost certainly depressed. It might be presumed that people with HIV infection would worry about their health all the time but the majority do not. Such worries are a stronger indication of psychiatric problems than anything else.[2,23] Complaints about cognitive problems in the absence of any measurable effects are also a strong indicator of depression rather than of actual cognitive decline.[24]

Previous personal loss

Previous losses in a person's life are important, but must be put into context. It is both true and important that people with AIDS suffer tremendous losses in their social circle, but this should be considered in comparison to groups with other illnesses. The study in Brazil compared men with leukaemias and lymphomas with men with HIV infection,[22] and the former group also reported many personal losses. They were admitted to wards where they made strong friendships with people also undertaking major treatments such as chemotherapy, and they lost these companions in the same way as people with HIV infection. Losses of these kinds are not a specific predictor for patients with HIV infection, but may be predictive for anyone with a terminal illness.

Carers

Caring for a partner or for someone who is sick is also a strong predictor of depression, particularly when the carer also has HIV infection.[25]

Life events

Although the role of life events and social support has been extensively researched, the findings have been rather meagre. Clearly, on an individual level, social support is important for patients in terms of quality of life and well-being, but this has not yielded easily to empirical research. There are many difficulties in studying the effects of life events and social support, not least in defining what is meant by 'social support' or to separate life events which are the cause or consequence of psychiatric disorder.[26] Specific life events and chronic stress have been regarded as important predictors of physical and psychological deterioration in HIV infection in some studies,[27] but not in others.[28]

Final thoughts

Does all this matter? Do stress and psychiatric problems lead to reduced immunocompetence and poorer physical outcome for patients? The answer is probably 'no'. It does not appear that major stress or psychological problems lead to impaired immunological function, but studies are hampered by all sorts of factors: which immunological test is performed, what does the test mean in terms of the disease, what about the psychiatric status and substance abuse, and the age, sex and health of the patient? All these factors obscure research into links between immunocompetence and psychiatric stress. None of this, however, negates the importance of recognising and treating psychiatric problems in people with HIV infection. Most of the depressive and adjustment difficulties, as well as the more serious psychotic states, are amenable to sensitive and effective intervention.

References

1. Dilley JW, Ochitill HN, Perl M, Volberding PA. Findings in psychiatric consultations with patients with acquired immune deficiency syndrome. *American Journal of Psychiatry* 1985; **142**: 82–6
2. King MB. Psychosocial status of 192 out-patients with HIV infection and AIDS. *British Journal of Psychiatry* 1989; **154**: 237–42
3. Joseph JG, Caumartin SM, Tal M, Kirscht JP, *et al.* Psychological functioning in a cohort of gay men at risk for AIDS. *Journal of Nervous and Mental Diseases* 1990; **178**: 607–15
4. Pergami A, Gala C, Burgess A, Durbano F, *et al.* The psychosocial impact of HIV infection in women. *Journal of Psychiatric Research* 1993; **37**: 687–96
5. Mellers JDC, Marchand-Gonod N, King MB, Laupa V, Smith JR. Mental health of women with HIV infection: a study in Paris and London. *European Psychiatry* (in press)
6. Perry S, Jacobsberg LB, Fishman B, Weiler PH, *et al.* Psychological responses to serological testing for HIV. *AIDS* 1990; **4**: 145–52
7. Atkinson Jr JH, Grant I, Kennedy CJ, Richman DD, *et al.* Prevalence of psychiatric disorders among men infected with human immunodeficiency virus. *Archives of General Psychiatry* 1988; **45**: 859–64
8. Marzuk PM, Tierney H, Tardiff K, Gross EM, *et al.* Increased risk of suicide in persons with AIDS. *Journal of the American Medical Association* 1988; **259**: 1333–7
9. Van den Boom FMLG, Mead C, Gremmen T, Roozenberg H. *AIDS, euthanasia and grief.* Paper presented at the VIIth International Conference on AIDS, Florence, 1991. Book of abstracts, vol 1, MD 55

10. Miller D, Acton TMG, Hedge B. The worried well: their identification and management. *Journal of the Royal College of Physicians of London* 1988; **22**:158–65

11. Kieburtz K, Zettelmaier AE, Ketonen L, Tuite M, Caine ED. Manic syndrome in AIDS. *American Journal of Psychiatry* 1991;**148**: 1068–70

12. Grant I, Atkinson H, Hesselink JR, Kennedy CR, *et al.* Evidence for early central nervous system involvement in the acquired immunodeficiency syndrome (AIDS) and other human immunodeficiency virus (HIV) infections. *Annals of Internal Medicine* 1987; **107**: 828–36

13. Harter DH. Neuropsychological status of asymptomatic individuals seropositive to HIV-1. *Annals of Neurology* 1989; **26**: 589–91

14. Wilkins JW, Robertson KR, Snyder CR, Robertson WK, *et al.* Implications of self-reported cognitive and motor dysfunction in HIV-positive patients. *American Journal of Psychiatry* 1991; **148**: 641–3

15. McArthur JC, Cohen BA, Selnes OA, Kumar AJ, *et al.* Low prevalence of neurological and neuropsychological abnormalities in otherwise healthy HIV-1 infected individuals: results from the multicenter AIDS cohort study. *Annals of Neurology* 1989; **26**: 601–11

16. Franzblau A, Letz R, Hershman D, Mason P, *et al.* Quantitative neurologic and neurobehavioral testing of persons infected with human immunodeficiency virus type 1. *Archives of Neurology* 1991; **48**: 263–8

17. Maj M. Mild cognitive dysfunction in physically asymptomatic HIV infection: recent research evidence and professional implications. *European Psychiatry* 1993; **8**: 173–7

18. World Health Organisation. *Global program on AIDS: report on the second consultation on the neuropsychiatric aspects of HIV-1 infection.* Ref. no. WHO/GPA/MNH/90.1. Geneva: WHO, 1990

19. Report of the Working Group of the American Academy of Neurology Task Force. Nomenclature and research definitions for neurologic manifestations of human immunodeficiency virus-type 1 (HIV-1) infection. *Neurology* 1991;**41**: 778–85

20. Everall IP, Luthert PJ, Lantos PL. Neuronal loss in the frontal cortex in HIV infection. *Lancet* 1991; **337**: 1119–21

21. Ellis D, Collis I, King M. A controlled comparison of HIV and general medical referrals to a liaison psychiatry service. *AIDS Care* 1994; **6**: 69–76

22. Caputi C, King M. *Psychological problems in men with HIV infection in Brazil: a controlled study.* Research report, University Department of Academic Psychiatry, Royal Free Hospital School of Medicine, 1994

23. Ostrow DG, Monjan A, Joseph J, van Raden M, *et al.* HIV-related symptoms and psychological functioning in a cohort of homosexual men. *American Journal of Psychiatry* 1989; **146**: 737–42

24. Herns M, Newman S, McAllister R, Weller I, Harrison M. *Mood state, neuropsychology and self reported cognitive deficits in HIV infection.* Paper presented at the Vth International Conference on AIDS, Montreal, 1989

25. McCann K, Wadsworth E. The role of informal carers in supporting gay men who have HIV related illness: what do they do and what are their needs? *AIDS Care* 1992; **4**: 25–34

26. Alloway R, Bebbington P. The buffer theory of social support — a review of the literature. *Psychological Medicine* 1987;**17**: 91–108

27. Rabkin JG, Williams JBW, Neugebauer R, Remien RH, Goetz R. Maintenance of hope in HIV-spectrum homosexual men. *American Journal of Psychiatry* 1990;**147**: 1322–6

28. Kessler RC, Foster C, Joseph J, Ostrow D, *et al.* Stressful life events and symptom onset in HIV infection. *American Journal of Psychiatry* 1991; **148**: 733–8

4 | Stroke

Graham P Mulley
Professor of Medicine for the Elderly, St James's University Hospital, Leeds

Allan House
Consultant and Senior Lecturer, Department of Liaison Psychiatry, The General Infirmary at Leeds

When doctors write of their personal experiences of stroke, they often highlight psychological features which have tended to be overlooked in formal medical education. The neuro-anatomist Brodal noted that he soon became tired when talking, reading or doing mental work.[1] His powers of concentration diminished, as did his short-term memory and initiative. Smithells described stroke as a 'cutting off of confidence' and felt a blow to his ego at not being able to move his limbs when he wanted.[2] Howell found everyday activities, such as putting on socks and trousers, exasperating:

> one of my greatest enemies was the frustration which resulted from fruitless struggling to perform tasks which would have normally been simple to carry out unaided. It could cause one to become morose and miserable.[3]

Mead's frustrations were related to loss of language:

> persons with the best of intentions keep putting words in your mouth — sometimes the wrong ones.[4]

He found that he was treated like an idiot, ignored or shouted at, and that people did things for him that were within his capabilities.

In reviewing the psychological manifestations of stroke, the focus will first be on these everyday problems of mood and cognition which are so important to patients' well-being. Specific diagnosable disorders of mood and cognitive problems will then be addressed, the latter often being related to the side, site and size of the vascular lesion and sometimes to the number of strokes a person has sustained.

The common psychological sequelae of stroke

Mood

Distress. After stroke there is an upsurge in symptoms best regarded as those of unhappiness or distress — sadness and tearfulness,

physical anxiety, insomnia and so on. These symptoms often do
not amount to a diagnosable mood disorder and are akin to those
of grieving. Like grief, their onset may be immediate or may occur
after a sort of honeymoon — perhaps after discharge from hospital
or when some other social experience makes the loss 'real' for the
stroke survivor.

Fatigue. In a survey of nearly 100 older Swedish stroke patients
followed up for two years, 21 stated that tiredness was one of
the main reasons for the decline in their quality of life.[5] A study
of younger Finnish stroke survivors found that, despite a good
recovery and return to work, quality of life (as judged by subjective
well-being) had not returned to its pre-stroke level in most subjects, two-thirds of the study group complaining of tiredness. The
nature of this symptom is unclear, but certainly it may prevent a
patient being actively involved in intensive rehabilitation for long
periods.

Worry. A particular worry is about having another stroke.[6] Physicians must remember to reassure people that secondary prevention (blood pressure control; aspirin; warfarin for those with atrial
fibrillation) can do much to reduce the risk of further episodes
and to remove the widespread false belief that 'the third stroke
always kills'.

Irritability. The difficulty of stroke patients in withstanding stress,
particularly noise (which can particularly upset those with dysphasia) should be remembered by ward staff. The haven of a quiet
room away from bleeps, telephones, televisions and general
conversation, is unfortunately not always available in hospital
wards.

Frustration. Being asked to do things that the patient is incapable of
doing, helped to do things he can easily do himself, and not able
to do or say those things that he used to do or say can be causes of
great distress. Many stroke patients swear — not so much because
of disinhibition but usually as a safety valve to release pent-up frustration. The desperation of some patients (especially those whose
language difficulties are poorly understood or badly handled by
care givers) can cause 'catastrophic reactions'. Here, frustration
and anger build up to an overwhelming degree, and the hapless
patient breaks down into sobbing or tears, reflecting hopelessness
and rage.[7]

Cognition

The ability to think logically, to judge, plan and take initiatives are important in rehabilitation and recovery but has not been adequately researched in stroke patients. Family and staff may not be prepared for illogical thinking or impulsive behaviour. Other important aspects of cognitive function have received little attention.

Memory. Some loss of memory occurs in most patients; recall of recent verbal material is a particular problem.[8] Patients should be reassured that this is common and does not imply senility. It is not known how memory impairment affects everyday life or how patients and relatives adapt to it.

Attention and concentration. These, too, may present obstacles to rehabilitation. Patients may be less alert or have problems with selection and orientation. Current measures of attention do not relate to everyday functioning and are of uncertain validity.

Specific psychological disorders which follow stroke

Mood disorders

Against the background of undifferentiated distress and emotional disturbance outlined above, a number of people develop more specific diagnosable mood disorders. The commonest are major depression, generalised anxiety, agoraphobia and pathological emotionalism (emotional lability).[9,10]

The importance of identifying these disorders is twofold: first, without identifying them it is easy to attribute poor outcomes to 'understandable distress' or 'personality change', so that an inaccurate prognosis is given. Secondly, the presence of specific diagnosable mood disorder can be an indication for specific treatments, for example:

- major depression is the most reliable indication for anti-depressive medication;
- agoraphobia (which can be readily mistaken for lack of motivation) may respond to behaviour therapy; and
- anxiety and its attendant problems may respond to a brief talking therapy.

The importance of these mood disorders is that they are a major component of quality of life for the stroke survivor. They influence physical and functional outcomes — probably through reducing the patient's capacity to participate actively in rehabilitation —

they can exacerbate cognitive problems, and are associated with poor family and social outcomes.

Cognitive disorders

Perceptual problems. As a general rule, stroke patients with weakness of the left side of the body are more likely to have difficulties interpreting sensory input to the brain. Damage to the right parietal lobe can cause difficulty understanding the affected side or the external environment.

Agnosia for body image[11] can cover a range of faulty perceptions: a feeling that the left arm is heavier or shorter than it should be; that there is a phantom extra arm; that one's arm does not belong to oneself — that it is someone else's, or that it is not an arm at all but a dog or a piece of meat. It is a kindness to explain that many people with left-sided weakness experience strange sensations in their left limbs, and to ask the patient to express them. This will relieve patients of the fear that they are going insane and increase trust in the understanding clinician.

Agnosia for external space may cause a patient to leave half a meal on the left side of the plate, be unable to find the way around once familiar terrain, and have problems distinguishing right from left, up from down and east from west. An awareness that these problems have a neurological explanation will prevent staff making mistaken judgemental comments about the patient's mental state.

Language difficulties. One verse of Psalm 137 says:

> If I forget thee, O Jerusalem, may my right hand wither . . . let my tongue cleave to the roof of my mouth;

The psalmist not only echoed the widespread belief that stroke is punishment for sin (it might be explained to patients that cerebrovascular disease is a reflection of the state of one's circulation rather than of one's soul), but he also made the observation that paralysis of the right hand may be associated with speech and language impairment. Such a complex function as language cannot be compartmentalised easily and no classification is entirely satisfactory. However, a system based on anatomy and clinical features can be used as a helpful guide.

In *non-fluent dysphasia* (also known as motor, expressive or Broca's dysphasia) the lesion is in Broca's area, in the left frontal lobe adjacent to the motor strip supplying the upper limb. The patient, whose right arm is weak, finds talking an effort and is often frustrated with the small output of meaningful words. These patients are all too aware of their language limitations.

In *fluent dysphasia* (sensory, receptive or Wernicke's dysphasia) the lesion is in the temporoparietal area, some distance from the motor strip. These patients may therefore have no arm weakness. They may start off a sentence normally but then seem to lose the thread of what they are saying. They speak a lot but say little, they may use circumlocutions or jargon, or be oblivious to their communication disorder. The history of the sudden onset of a change in language helps distinguish these stroke patients from those with psychotic problems.

Global dysphasia occurs when a large part of the left hemisphere is damaged. The unfortunate patient may be able to make only sounds or simple words — although sometimes surprising people with automatic speech and by an ability to sing word perfect (music being a function of the right hemisphere).

Confusional states. Stroke may cause acute confusion (now called delirium) or dementia. In a survey of 145 consecutive cases of acute stroke, 48% were confused on admission or in the first few days.[12] Delirium was more common in older people, in those with extensive paralysis or who had previously had a delirium state, and in those treated with anticholinergic drugs. Specific symptoms may be seen which relate to the arterial territory involved, for example:

- stroke in the anterior cerebral artery region can cause sexual disinhibition and irrational behaviour;
- stroke in the part of the brain supplied by the middle cerebral artery (which is the most commonly involved) may produce agitation; and
- forced shouting has been described in posterior circulation strokes.

Delirium. Strokes constitute the second commonest cause of dementia. Permanent cognitive impairment occurs in one in ten of those who survive to six months.[13] Typically, those with multiple bilateral lesions are more likely to become demented. Patients with vascular dementia have more thalamic infarcts than non-demented stroke patients.[14] Post-stroke dementia is not necessarily the result of multiple infarctions: 'mono-infarct' dementia also occurs. Vascular dementia is generally more distressing for the patient than Alzheimer's disease because the former patient (whose mental and physical capabilities may vary from day to day) is more likely to have insight into his or her mental deterioration. This can also compound the patient's depression.

Factors associated with psychological disorder after stroke

It is not always easy to see why one person develops significant psychiatric problems after stroke while another does not, but there are some general pointers as to those at risk. First, those with a history of previous psychiatric disorder or with psychiatric disorder at the time of stroke are obviously at risk. This particular type of lightning does strike twice in the same place.

Secondly, the individual's social context can be a source of vulnerability or of protection. A substantial proportion of patients will have experienced some other major stressor in the year before their stroke.[15] Social support is an important factor in protecting against stresses — yet a third of old people live alone.

Stroke is a *family* disease, and the impact on the relatives is centrally important. Spouses experience a modified bereavement reaction after stroke. They too suffer anxiety, depression, irritability and tiredness. There are problems with role change, guilt, sexual expression and marital strain. Time taken to listen to family carers, to give them information about stroke, to explain that their experiences are not unique and to be available for counselling and advice can be helpful. Relatives' support groups also have an important role.

Thirdly, biological factors and the localisation of the stroke lesion may be important. Cognitive impairment can interact with mood disturbances so that each contributes to a complex dysfunction while either alone might not be of clinical severity. The lesion localisation is important in determining specific cognitive deficits, but its role in mood disorders is less clear cut.[16]

Conclusion

An awareness of the psychological effects of stroke is important if we are to understand our patients, help them to understand themselves, and provide the optimum ambience for rehabilitation, recovery and adaptation. The good clinician will make time to listen and explain, and will avoid making judgemental comments about those stroke patients who are distressed or who do not appear to be behaving appropriately.

The main aims of the clinical assessment of stroke patients are threefold:

1. To identify psychological problems, in particular those specific psychiatric syndromes which may be amenable to treatment.
2. To identify those patients at most risk of developing psychiatric problems — especially those with social vulnerabilities and/or psychiatric histories.
3. To look for clues in poorer-than-expected outcomes which might point to unidentified psychological problems. A useful pointer here for the experienced clinician is a gap between *impairment* (which is usually related to disease severity) and *disability* or *handicap* (which has a major psychological component).

It is only through integrating physical and psychological aspects of assessment and treatment in this way that good quality stroke care can be provided — either in the specialist stroke unit or in the general medical setting.

References

1. Brodal A. Self-observations and neuroanatomical considerations after a stroke. *Brain* 1973; **96**: 675–94
2. Smithells P. A personal account by a sufferer from a stroke. *New Zealand Medical Journal* 1978; **87**: 396–7
3. Howell TH. How my teaching about the management of stroke would change after my own. *British Medical Journal* 1984; **289**: 35–7
4. Mead S. The doctor has a stroke. *Lancet* 1963; **ii**: 574–6
5. Ahsio B, Britton M, Murray V, Theorell T. Disablement and quality of life after stroke. *Stroke* 1984; **15**: 886–900
6. Niemi M-L, Laaksonen R, Kotila M, Wattimo O. Quality of life four years after stroke. *Stroke* 1988; **19**: 1101–7
7. Benson DF. Psychiatric aspects of aphasia. *British Journal of Psychiatry* 1973; **123**: 555–6
8. Hier DB, Mondlock J, Caplan JR. Behavioural abnormalities after right hemisphere stroke. *Neurology* 1983; **33**: 337–44
9. House A, Dennis M, Mogridge L, Warlow C, *et al.* Mood disorders in the first year after stroke. *British Journal of Psychiatry* 1991; **158**: 83–92
10. House A, Dennis M, Warlow C, Hawton K. Emotionalism after stroke. *British Medical Journal* 1989; **298**: 991–4
11. Cutting J. Study of anosognosia. *Journal of Neurology, Neurosurgery and Psychiatry* 1978; **41**: 548–55
12. Gustafson Y, Olsson T, Eriksson S, Asplund K, Bucht G. Acute confusional states (delirium) in stroke patients. *Cerebrovascular Diseases* 1991; **1**: 257–64
13. Ebrahim S, Nuori F, Barer D. Cognitive impairment after stroke. *Age and Ageing* 1985; **14**: 345–50
14. Ladburner G, Iliff LD, Lechner H. Clinical factors associated with

dementia in ischaemic stroke. *Journal of Neurology, Neurosurgery and Psychiatry* 1982; **45**: 97–101

15. House A, Dennis M, Mogridge L, Hawton K, Warlow C. Stressful life events and difficulties in the year preceding stroke: a case control study. *Journal of Neurology, Neurosurgery and Psychiatry* 1990; **53**: 1024–8

16. House A, Dennis M, Warlow C, Hawton K, Molyneux A. Mood disorders after stroke and their relation to lesion location: a CT scan study. *Brain* 1990; **113**: 1113–29

Part 2
From recognition to intervention

There is no discontinuity between non-specialist and specialist psychiatric care. Everybody has some psychological needs which should be met by a good health care system, and the first steps in treating any psychiatric disorder are taken by a non-specialist. On the other hand, there is more to psychological therapies than common sense and being nice to people. Therapies can be delivered according to definite psychological principles which can be defined and taught; this is important because psychological problems tend to improve only if they are addressed specifically by effective therapies.

In this section, the *basics of psychological care* are first discussed from the two perspectives of working in a large cancer hospital and the management of coronary artery disease. Perhaps the key message is that psychological care is not something which is 'done' to people, neither is it passive or accepting like so much ill-defined counselling and support: it is interactive and interrogative. The aim is always to engage the patient in dialogue, to elicit his concerns — realistic and otherwise — and to 'negotiate' with him. This approach may be unfamiliar and uncomfortable to those untrained in psychological therapies, but it is rarely unappreciated by patients and has been shown to be effective in many trials. It can also sit easily in the medical milieu, where time is of the essence and much communication is conversational rather than traditionally psychotherapeutic in style.

Chapter 6 indicates the role of *psychological* treatments in modifying misconceptions and inappropriate details which result in "disproportionate" disability in a minority of patients. Such methods can often be simple and make considerable use of well planned self help materials but may occasionally require referral to a psychologist or psychiatrist.

Drug therapies are then discussed. They are frequently used, but often misused. What are the main indications for antidepressants, how should a rational therapeutic trial be conducted and which drug might be chosen? There need be no conflict between a

39

psychological and a medical approach to treatment, and the rational use of psychotropic drugs is an important skill in the general hospital as it is in psychiatric practice elsewhere.

It is our belief that these chapters outline basic principles of psychological and pharmacological therapy. As such, practising clinicians should be familiar enough with them to apply them in their routine work. In addition only a minority of medical patients will see a psychiatrist, so the physician has to make important decisions about psychiatric referral:

- where the responsibility lies for psychological care — with the GP or the hospital
- what psychological skills the physician should possess;
- how to handle psychiatric referral; and
- what to expect from psychiatric referral.

Once these decisions are made, then the appropriate clinical services can be planned and implemented. That is the topic of the third section of this book.

5 | Improving the psychological care of cancer patients

Peter Maguire
Director and Honorary Consultant Psychiatrist, Cancer Research Campaign Psychological Medicine Group, Christie Hospital, Manchester

Anthony Howell
Consultant Medical Oncologist, Christie Hospital, Manchester

If cancer patients are to avoid developing generalised anxiety disorders, major depressive illness or adjustment disorders, they have to come to terms with certain hurdles which arise as a result of their diagnosis or treatment. Unfortunately, a substantial minority fail to do so, and at least one-third of cancer patients develop psychological or psychiatric morbidity within two years of diagnosis. Few of those affected are recognised as needing help and treated appropriately. The aim of this chapter, therefore, is to discuss the hurdles that cancer patients have to overcome, the psychological and psychiatric morbidity which results if they fail to do so, the reasons why little of this morbidity is recognised and treated appropriately, and ways of reducing and preventing it.

The likelihood of patients developing psychological and psychiatric morbidity has been found to be proportional to the number of their undisclosed and unresolved concerns.[1] It is therefore important that health professionals are aware of the key hurdles with which patients have to try to come to terms.

Hurdles related to illness

Uncertainty

Many cancer patients have experienced cancer in a close friend or relative. They are aware, therefore, that their disease could recur at any time and cause premature death. While many patients remain optimistic about their prognosis, some become plagued by worry that their cancer will return — a worry that is fuelled by articles in newspapers and magazines and by programmes on television. If patients have constant reminders that they have had treatment for

41

cancer, like a scar or loss of a crucial body function, this may also remind them of their predicament.

Search for meaning

It is easier for individuals to cope with life-threatening events if they can find an adequate explanation for their position. Clear risk factors have been identified for illnesses like coronary heart disease, but few have been found for cancer. This leaves a vacuum into which patients can project their own theories. They may either blame themselves, and attribute having cancer to some flaw in their personality or an inability to handle stress, or blame other people (eg their partners). When patients blame themselves or others, it is much harder for them to adapt to the cancer diagnosis and treatment.

Contributing to survival

Most patients adapt better if they feel there is something they can contribute towards ensuring their own survival. Given the absence of risk factors, it is difficult to know what they can do to prevent relapse. Some patients turn to psychological methods like meditation or relaxation, while others turn to healthier diets and lifestyles. As long as these strategies are kept within reasonable bounds patients cope better than those who feel there is nothing they can do to contribute to their survival.

Maintaining self esteem

It is postulated that some cancers are caused by infection, for example, by slow viruses, so it is not surprising that some patients believe that having cancer makes them contagious and unclean. This can lead them to feel stigmatised and to believe that they are not as acceptable to other people as before their illness. Such feelings of stigma are especially likely when their cancer has been associated with causes like promiscuity (as in the case of cancer of the cervix).

Being open with others

Patients who are open with their partners, close friends and other relatives fare better psychologically than those who keep their predicament secret or confide only in their partner. However, there is a realistic risk for some patients that being open with an employer about cancer may have a detrimental effect on their career prospects.

Maintaining contact with others

Cancer and cancer treatments are not comfortable topics to talk about to other people. Friends and relatives may begin to avoid the cancer patient because they are frightened of upsetting the patient or saying the wrong thing. Moreover, they may not wish to hear how unpleasant the treatment is or that the cancer has not responded to treatment. Therefore, while the cancer experience may bring patients closer to partners, friends and relatives, it may also lead to increasing separation. The resulting isolation makes it hard for the cancer patient to cope.

Obtaining medical support

Common sense would suggest that the cancer patient would be given considerable support as a result of diagnosis and treatment. However, for reasons that will be discussed later, there is a tendency for doctors, nurses and other health professionals to distance themselves from the cancer patient because they find it difficult to cope with certain aspects of the patient's predicament. The absence of such on-going support renders patients more vulnerable to psychiatric breakdown, particularly to the development of an affective disorder.

Key questions about hurdles

The risk of patients developing clinical anxiety or depression is much greater if they fail to negotiate any of these seven key hurdles. In assessing a cancer patient early after diagnosis it is therefore useful to ask key questions to elicit how he or she is managing each of them.

These questions should include the following:

- 'How do you see your illness working out?'
- 'Have you been able to come up with any explanation as to why you should have become ill in this way?'
- 'Have you found there is anything you have been able to do to contribute towards your survival?'
- 'Has having cancer changed in any way how you feel about yourself as a person?'

- 'Have you been able to be open with others about having cancer?'
- 'Have you been seeing as much of other people as you did before your illness?'
- 'How do you feel about the level of support you have been receiving from the doctors and nurses who have been looking after you?'

When patients' responses indicate that they have not managed to overcome one or more of these hurdles it is important to explore further to see if there are any signs and symptoms of an anxiety state and/or depressive illness.

Hurdles related to treatment

Loss of body part or function

Patients also have to come to terms with treatments which result in the loss of either a body part (eg loss of a breast after mastectomy) or an important bodily function (eg loss of bowel function after a colostomy for anorectal cancer). Up to a quarter of patients undergoing such surgery develop persisting body image problems. There is a strong link between this and later affective disorders, so it is important to ask patients routinely how they have felt about losing a particular body part or function. If there are body image problems, questions should be asked to check whether these have led to anxiety and depression.

Radiotherapy and chemotherapy

Many patients undergo radiotherapy and/or chemotherapy. There is a direct link between the number and severity of adverse effects caused by these treatments and the risk of affective disorders. It is therefore important to enquire whether the patient has been experiencing any adverse effects and how serious these have been. There is also a strong link between the development of conditioned responses after chemotherapy and later psychiatric problems. The possibility of conditioning having developed should be explored by asking patients about any effects the chemotherapy has been having.

Radiotherapy may lead to loss of sexual functioning through, for example, ablation of the ovaries. If this has occurred, the effects on the patient's sexual functioning need to be established. Similarly, chemotherapy can affect sexual functioning by its effects on the hormones that drive sexual functioning and sexuality, and patients may experience a loss of libido and become sterile or infertile.

Surgical complications like lymphoedema after mastectomy, which cause swelling and pain and hinder full recovery, can make patients more vulnerable to affective disorders. Major abdominal surgery, for example, as in the formation of a colostomy for anorectal cancer, can result in damage to the nerve supply of the sexual organs and result in profound sexual problems for both men and women.

Psychological and psychiatric morbidity

Given these hurdles relating both to diagnosis and to treatment, it is not surprising that studies consistently find a substantial psychological and psychiatric morbidity in patients with cancer. Between 25% and 33% of cancer patients develop a generalised anxiety disorder, major depressive illness or adjustment disorder within the first two years of diagnosis.[2] Body image problems occur in up to 25% of those who lose an important body part or function, whilst sexual problems affect 25–33% of patients. Confusional states may be found in 10–40%, and are usually due to cancer progression, associated biochemical changes like hypercalcaemia, brain metastases, the use of certain drugs or opportunistic infections.[3] Overall, therefore, there is substantial psychological and psychiatric morbidity associated with cancer — at least three to four times greater than would be expected in a sample of people from the community matched by age and gender.

Detection of psychological and psychiatric morbidity

Cohort studies have found that only a small proportion of patients who develop morbidity are recognised and treated. In a study of breast cancer patients only 20% of those who developed anxiety, depression, or sexual or body image problems were recognised and offered help by the surgical team or the general practitioner (GP). Nurses were no more likely than doctors to elicit which patients needed help. Similarly, a study of patients with cervical cancer found that only a quarter of women who became anxious and depressed were so recognised. Even in a medical oncology unit where there was an established liaison psychiatry service only 40% of the patients who needed psychiatric help were recognised as needing it.[4] The detection rates are even lower when more subtle psychological problems are considered. Only 15% of patients with body image problems are detected, whilst sexual difficulties are recognised rarely (9%). It is therefore important to consider why so little morbidity is detected, despite the growing awareness of its existence and the dedication of doctors and nurses to the care of cancer patients.

Reasons for hidden morbidity

Patient led

Patients are reluctant to disclose the problems mentioned above because they believe they are an inevitable consequence of being diagnosed and treated for cancer. They wrongly consider that they cannot be alleviated and see no point in mentioning them. Moreover, the more they like and respect the doctors and nurses involved in their care the less they wish to burden them. They worry that time taken up with these psychological problems means that less attention will be paid to ensuring their physical survival. Some patients are also afraid they will be judged as inadequate in their personalities if they admit they are struggling to cope.

Patients also implicate the behaviour of health professionals when they claim that if they give verbal ('I have been upset') or non-verbal cues (begin to cry) they are met by distancing strategies from the health professional (eg 'I can see you are getting upset, you're bound to be at this stage, but everything will be all right').

Doctor led

Objective scrutiny of the performance of doctors and nurses in talking with cancer patients has highlighted three findings.[2] First, doctors and nurses avoid focusing on psychosocial aspects. Thus, it is rare for them to ask women after mastectomy how they feel about losing a breast. Secondly, when patients volunteer information about both physical and psychosocial aspects health professionals attend selectively to the physical aspects. If a patient says he is having trouble with sickness because of chemotherapy, is feeling very fatigued and worrying about his future, the doctor or nurse will tend to explore the first two aspects and ignore his worry about the future.

Thirdly, if faced with this behaviour, patients persist in giving further cues that they have psychological problems which they wish to discuss, then distancing strategies will be used by the health professional which are designed to keep the conversation in neutral and safe waters.

Distancing strategies by health professionals

Normalisation

The doctor or nurse may explain that the patient's distress is normal in the circumstances and will lessen over time.

Premature reassurance

Doctors and nurses are keen to help patients cope with their predicament. When they hear of a patient's concerns, they move quickly into reassurance mode in a bid to persuade the patient that things are likely to work out all right. If this is done before eliciting the patient's concerns, the patient will not heed the reassurance and keep key concerns hidden.

Premature advice

Similarly, there is a tendency for doctors or nurses to move rapidly into giving advice to patients about what they will be able to do before having fully explored their worries.

False reassurance

When faced with grave predicaments the doctor or nurse may be tempted to give false reassurance — that is, to pretend wrongly that the situation is better than it is — which will block further patient disclosure.

Passing the buck

Medical and nursing staff often feel that they do not have adequate information or the freedom to discuss matters fully with the patient. They will then be tempted to pass the buck by saying that it would be better to ask the consultant when he comes on the ward round tomorrow.

Switching the subject

When suddenly faced with a difficult issue the health professional may deliberately or unwittingly change the subject. For example, when the doctor asks how the patient is feeling, the latter may say that he feels exhausted and is beginning to think that he is not going to get better. He then asks the doctor whether he *is* going to get better — to which the doctor will reply by asking how his breathing has been.

Jollying along

When nursing staff notice that a patient is particularly gloomy or anxious, they may try to jolly him along by saying that there is no need to look so glum — it is a lovely day outside. These distancing tactics are used commonly by all health professionals and it is important to consider the reasons.

Reasons for distancing

In-depth interviews with experienced doctors and nurses have revealed important reasons why they distance themselves from patients' emotions and for their reluctance to probe into psychological and social aspects.

They fear that such enquiry will unleash strong emotions like anger or despair, with which they will have neither the time nor the skill to deal. Health professionals are especially afraid that these emotions, inadequately dealt with, will damage the patients pyschologically, and that they might lose all hope.

They worry that entering into effective dialogue with patients will increase the risk of being asked difficult questions (eg 'am I dying?', 'how long have I got?', or even 'why didn't you diagnose it sooner?'). It could also result in them finding out the true extent of the patients' and family's suffering, both physically and emotionally. If this happened too often, doctors and nurses could begin to suffer themselves, which might jeopardise their own ability to make decisions about treatment and affect their personal survival. They also worry that psychological enquiry will take up too much time in busy clinics and prevent them paying sufficient attention to physical aspects of the disease.

When questioned further about why they have such strong fears, health professionals highlight the lack of training in key assessment skills and, in particular, how to explore patients' feelings and move on reasonably quickly to other topics. They emphasise how little training they have had in handling difficult situations like breaking bad news, answering difficult questions and helping patients manage the inevitable uncertainty associated with cancer diagnosis.

Some experienced doctors and nurses also highlight the lack of support for a more psychological way of working.

The development of other approaches

The traditional liaison psychiatry approach has relied on clinicians to decide which patients require referral to the psychiatric service. For the reasons discussed earlier, this approach leads to a minority of those patients who need help receiving it. An attempt was therefore made to determine whether training specialist nurses in counselling and monitoring skills would lead to a much higher recognition and referral rate, with a consequent reduction in psychiatric morbidity.

Intervention scheme

We conducted a study in which 152 patients about to undergo mastectomy were randomised either to counselling or to monitoring by a specially trained nurse or to routine care alone. The nurses were trained to provide information and advice before and after surgery, and then to visit each patient in their home every two months for the first year after mastectomy. The psychological and social adjustment of the patients was assessed at the time of surgery, and three and 12–18 months later by trained interviewers using standardised interview schedules and diagnostic criteria.

The specialist nurses were able to recognise 90% of those who developed an affective disorder, body image or sexual problem, in contrast to 15% recognised by the doctors and nurses looking after those women assigned to the control group; 76% of those requiring referral in the specialist nurse arm were so referred compared with 15% in the control group. Consequently, there was a more than threefold difference in psychiatric morbidity in favour of the specialist nurse arm (12%) compared with the control arm (39%).[5]

There were, however, problems with this intervention scheme. Following up every patient on a two-monthly basis caused some of them to worry more than they would have done had they been left alone. They preferred to put concerns about their predicament to the back of their minds. Being visited by a nurse reactivated their worries and made them much more concerned. Some patients became dependent on the nurse and looked to her to help them with worries unrelated to cancer or treatment. The nurse was inevitably faced with an accumulating load of patients since she had to continue to monitor each of them for one year.

Limited intervention scheme

To overcome these problems we developed a system which sought to limit the involvement of the specialist nurses. They were required simply to assess once each mastectomy patient at home after surgery, but to do so in a way that educated patients to realise that they were allowed and encouraged to disclose any psychological or psychiatric problems that developed. When problems were already apparent, the nurse referred the patient to the back-up psychiatric team or to the patient's GP. If no problems were evident, the nurse explained to the patient that she should feel free to contact her if problems arose over the next few months.

A third condition was included which involved training ward and community nurses in key assessment skills. Patients randomised to this condition were assessed before and after surgery by a ward nurse, and after discharge were referred on to an appropriate district nurse or health visitor. A trial was then carried out in which 186 patients were randomised to one of these three conditions:

- full intervention;
- limited intervention; or
- follow up by the ward and community nurses.

The limited intervention proved as effective as the full intervention scheme in picking up and referring those patients who needed help,[6] yet it was more cost-effective, and patients could be relied on to refer themselves if problems arose after the initial assessment. The ward and community arm failed, and many patients' problems went unrecognised and untreated. Ward nurses showed an increase in key skills as a result of feedback training, but failed to achieve clinical competence in the assessment of anxiety and depression. The community nurses proved reluctant to take on this psychological assessment role.

The limited intervention scheme is now the basis of the work of specialist cancer nurses in our health district and is being adopted widely elsewhere. It has the advantage of freeing the nurse to focus on those patients who need help and to carry out treatments such as anxiety management and cognitive behavioural therapy.

Training doctors and nurses

Relying on specialist nurses to deal with the psychosocial aspects of care carries an inherent danger, namely, that other health professionals may decide to leave all such care in their hands. It is therefore important to help experienced doctors and nurses in cancer care to upgrade their own psychological assessment skills and their ability to deal with difficult situations. We have established three- or five-day multidisciplinary residential workshops. They seek to help doctors and nurses relinquish their distancing strategies, acquire the key skills that promote patient disclosure, and enable them to become more confident at managing difficult situations like breaking bad news.[7] The key skills which inhibit and promote patient disclosure are shown in Table 1.

Table 1. Effect on patients' disclosure of key concerns.

Promote	Inhibit
Open directive questions	Leading questions
Questions with a psychological focus	Questions with a physical focus
Clarification of psychological aspects	Clarification of physical aspects
Summarising	Giving reassurance
Empathy	Giving advice
Making educated guesses	

Objective ratings of assessment interviews conducted by the 206 experienced doctors and nurses who have attended the workshops show that the ratio of behaviours which inhibited disclosure to those promoting disclosure was 1:3 — a ratio that held regardless of age, prior experience, professional discipline or current working situation.[8] It is therefore clear that health professionals involved in cancer care need help to relinquish their inhibitory behaviours and to acquire the skills that promote patient disclosure.

Screening for affective disorders

An alternative way of detecting those who need psychiatric help is to use screening instruments. Two such instruments that have been shown to be effective in screening out those with affective disorders are the Hospital Anxiety and Depression Scale and the Rotterdam Symptom Check-list.[9] However, even with the use of screening instruments two problems have been encountered: first, although patients may score above the relevant threshold indicating probable cases of anxiety and depression, there is no guarantee they will accept that they need help. Secondly, when a cohort of consecutive high scorers was followed up in our own service it proved difficult for specialist cancer nurses to interview all the high scorers to determine whether or not they were true cases. Consequently, the feasibility of screening in a busy cancer hospital must be questioned.

Preventing affective disorders

Recent research has established that one of the main determinants of the psychological adjustment of patients is whether or not they perceive that the information given at the time of the initial bad news consultation is adequate to their needs. Patients who believe they have had too much or too little information will perceive it as inadequate compared with patients who feel that the information was tailored to what they were ready for and wanted to know.

It has also been found that patients who have more concerns about their predicament, and which are not resolved, are more likely to develop anxiety or depression.[1,10] More effective handling of the bad news consultation and the eliciting of and responding to patients' concerns should lead to a marked reduction in the incidence of affective disorders.

Breaking bad news

The first step is to check if the patient is already aware that he has a malignant disease. This can best be achieved by asking him directly whether he has had any thoughts about what the diagnosis might be, and then exploring the reasons for this. Such questioning will usually reveal that he has come to an appropriate conclusion on the basis of his symptoms and past experience of cancer in others. It is then a matter of confirming that his awareness is correct.

When patients are unaware that they have cancer it is important to fire a warning shot to see if they wish to know more about their disease or prefer to leave it to the expert. This can best be done by saying 'I am afraid that it is not just a straightforward ulcer'. A patient can then indicate a wish either to pull out by saying 'that's all right, doctor, I'll leave the detail to you', or to continue further into the truth-telling process by asking what is meant by 'serious'. By using a hierarchy of euphemisms (eg 'serious', 'abnormal cells', 'kind of tumour', and 'cancer') it is possible to slow down the transition from the patient's perception of himself as being well to that of having a potentially life-threatening illness. Slowing down the bad news in this way reduces the risk that he will move into denial or become disorganised emotionally.

When the diagnosis has been confirmed or broken to the patient it is important to pause to give him a chance to assimilate the information and respond emotionally. The patient's upset should then be acknowledged and he be asked if he can bear to say what is making him so upset. This will reveal the key concerns provoked by the bad news, and the doctor is then in a position to ask the patient to put these in priority order and to respond to each in turn. In this way, the doctor maximises the likelihood of the patient assimilating the information in an appropriate manner, but he will also elicit the related concerns and associated feelings. The patient is then likely to feel satisfied with the amount of information given since it has been tailored to his needs. He will also have had his concerns heeded, if not resolved.

However well bad news is broken, the patient is likely to experience some difficulty in coming to terms with the inherent uncertainty of a cancer diagnosis. It is important to acknowledge this uncertainty by saying that it *is* uncertain and by empathising ('I can see this is very difficult for you'). The patient can then be asked whether he would prefer to have regular indicators of his disease status through regular investigation and feedback or to forget about it. It is also possible to negotiate with patients how frequently they would like follow-up appointments. Some patients want as few as possible because their worries are reactivated by visits to a cancer hospital; others like regular two- or three-monthly appointments because they start worrying about recurrence one or two months after a visit to the clinic.

Conclusion

Few doctors have received training in this mode of breaking bad news, and further research is needed to determine whether training them in the methods described above reduces affective disorders markedly. Meanwhile, the best way of delivering psychiatric care would seem to be to train and employ specialist nurses to continue their counselling and therapeutic activities with cancer patients and relatives, and to ensure that they have the necessary skills to recognise and refer patients for psychological and psychiatric help. Efforts should also continue to upgrade the assessment skills of clinicians and to encourage them to take on the treatment of disorders like anxiety and depression. Continued reliance on the conventional liaison psychiatry approach will make little impact on the substantial morbidity that has been discussed.

References

1. Parle M, Jones B, Maguire P. Maladaptive coping and affective disorder amongst cancer patients. (submitted to *Psychological Medicine*)
2. Maguire P. Improving the recognition of affective disorders in cancer patients. In: Grossman K, ed. *Recent advances in clinical psychiatry.* Edinburgh: Churchill Livingstone, 1992: 15–30
3. Goldberg RJ. Psychiatric aspects of psychosocial distress in cancer patients. *Journal of Psychosocial Oncology* 1988; **6:** 139–63
4. Hardman A, Maguire P, Crowther D. The recognition of psychiatric morbidity on a medical oncology ward. *Journal of Psychosomatic Research* 1989; **33:** 235–7
5. Maguire P, Tait A, Brooke M, Thomas C, Sellwood RA. Effective counselling on the psychiatric morbidity associated with mastectomy. *British Medical Journal* 1980; **281:** 1454–6
6. Wilkinson S, Maguire P, Tait A. Life after breast cancer. *Nursing Times* 1988; **54:** 34–7
7. Maguire P, Faulkner A. How to improve the counselling skills of doctors and nurses involved in cancer care. *British Medical Journal* 1988; **297:** 847–9
8 Maguire P, Booth K, Elliott C, Hillier V. Helping cancer patients disclose their concerns. (submitted to *European Journal of Cancer*)
9. Ibbotson T, Maguire P, Selby P, Priestman T, Wallace L. Screening for anxiety and depression in cancer patients. Effects of disease and treatment. *European Journal of Cancer* 1994; **30a:** 37–40
10. Parle M, Maguire P. Exploring the relationship between coping and the demands of cancer. *Journal of Psychosocial Oncology* (in press)

6 | The place of psychological therapies in coronary artery disease

Bob Lewin
Consultant Clinical Psychologist, Astley Ainslie Hospital, Edinburgh

The most obvious role for clinical psychologists who work with physically ill patients is to identify and treat psychological distress. This distress may be the result of receiving a serious diagnosis, because of painful or frightening symptoms or the results of side-effects from the medical treatment. Serious or protracted health problems are almost always associated with an increased incidence of anxiety, depression and, in a few illnesses, suicide. Even in the absence of a clinically diagnosable psychological 'illness', health problems may have psychological effects that significantly reduce the patient's quality of life; for example, by exacerbating or bringing about relationship and/or sexual problems, provoking undue illness behaviour or by causing a general loss of confidence or feelings of self worth. Standardised psychological treatments have been developed and empirically tested (through randomised controlled trials) for most of these problems. Some psychological problems yield to treatment more reliably than others, and work continues to find better ways to help patients and their physicians. (Incidentally, most clinical psychologists do not react well to being described as 'counsellors' or to being asked to apply some 'tender loving care' to a patient.)

Routine screening for and attending to such distress should be important elements in any humane treatment system. However, it will be argued here that, in any but the most acute or superficial of medical interventions, psychological factors play an important role in determining outcome. Indeed, in some cases, psychological factors may be the single most important variable contributing to the overall outcome. This will be illustrated through the example of coronary artery disease.

Impairment, disability and handicap

It is helpful to view a patient's presentation by dividing it into three aspects:

1. *Impairment:* the extent of the underlying lesion; the directly measurable damage (eg the extent of atheroma in the cardiac arteries). The level of measurement is empirical and highly reproducible.
2 *Disability:* the degree to which patients differ on normative, functional and adjustment measures from their age-matched contemporaries. This includes symptoms such as angina or tiredness and restricted functional abilities (walking, etc.) and also quality-of-life measures (mood, sleep disturbance, etc). Such measures may be highly variable from occasion to occasion and situation to situation.
3. *Handicap:* the sum of the impairment and the disability plus the additional burdens placed on the patient by society (eg employment problems through prejudice).

Obviously, the individual clinician cannot do much about society's handicapping notions, so the scope for therapeutic intervention is restricted to tackling impairment and disability. The treatment of chronic disease often proceeds on the assumption that, as in acute injury or illness, impairment and disability are strongly causally associated and that removing or reducing impairment will automatically serve to reduce or remove disability. Unfortunately, this is often not the case.

Impairment

The amelioration of impairment

In coronary artery disease, surgery and drugs can reduce symptoms and act as secondary prevention against further impairment. Perhaps the single biggest step forward in cardiac rehabilitation was taken by those brave doctors who, in the 1950s, allowed their post-myocardial infarction patients to get out of bed and sit in an armchair before the usual six weeks of total bed rest had elapsed! Subsequent research confirmed that this significantly reduced not only mortality but also psychological morbidity. A handful of enthusiasts sought to extend this approach by introducing formal exercise programmes for patients. They showed that many myocardial infarction patients could achieve a significant training effect but that, for some reason, restoring patients to their previous level of functional ability did not necessarily result in them taking advantage of it.

The relationship of impairment to disability

At the International Federation of Cardiology conference in Turku, Finland in 1975, a resolution was passed, albeit narrowly, which could be paraphrased as 'call in the shrinks: we need some help — we do not understand why these patients will not go back to work or resume their sexual life and why they seem so fearful'. It had become clear that, although many patients were left with little in the way of *impairment,* they still displayed a great deal of *disability.*

The lack of correlation between impairment and disability is also found in coronary artery disease patients who have not experienced the trauma of a myocardial infarction. For example, in a series of 50 cardiac catheterisation patients Smith *et al.*[1] showed that there was no significant relationship between the severity of the stenosis and the frequency or severity of anginal episodes, the degree to which these episodes interfered with the patient's activity or the degree to which the patient claimed that he avoided activity as the result of angina. There were, however, quite reasonable and significant correlations (typically = 0.4) between the number of angina episodes and psychological variables such as anger and anxiety.

Impairment and distress

Many studies have sought to determine the relationship between impairment and psychological distress (disability) in coronary artery disease, but none has found any significant relationship between the severity of the disease and the amount of psychological distress manifest by the patient.

Impairment and treatment success

A similar lack of relationship appears to exist between impairment and treatment outcome. An attempt was made at the Duke University Medical Center to build a computer model that could predict which patients, newly presenting to the clinic with angina and with angiographically established coronary artery disease, would report at six months that their treatment was successful.[2] A total of 101 medical variables were entered into this analysis. When patients with less severe coronary artery disease (70% occlusion of one artery) were removed from the analysis the only significant predictor left in the model was 'hypochondriasis' (an undue attention to symptoms and health matters), as measured by a simple questionnaire. Among the rejected medical variables were:

- the number and degree of ST-T wave changes seen on exercise testing;
- the number of occluded vessels;
- the site and degree of the stenosis;
- whether or not patients had left ventricular failure; and
- the ejection fraction.

In a new sample of patients, this computer model successfully predicted 85% of those who at six months would claim a lack of treatment success. The authors pointed out that most of these patients, having failed first-line medical treatment, would be offered elective coronary artery bypass surgery — despite the fact that, in the majority of cases, it was psychological not pathological factors that differentiated them from those who would not be offered surgery.

Psychological distress: cause or effect?

It may be that patients who fail to gain sufficient relief are more 'hypochondriacal' because the underlying impairment *is* worse, but measures such as angiography are too insensitive to reveal it. One way to approach this is to ask which comes first: the psychological distress or the symptoms? In a prospective study of 10,000 symptom-free Israeli men,[3] those patients who at baseline had reported raised levels of anxiety or a stressful lifestyle were twice as likely as those without such raised levels to have developed symptoms suggestive of angina at the five-year follow-up.

A number of recent studies have shown that in both animals and humans ischaemia can be elicited in the laboratory by a variety of psychological stressors. A growing number of studies are reporting an independent relationship between distress and early mortality. In the first year after myocardial infarction a mortality rate of 5–10% can be expected, but in the anxious and depressed sub-group, who are no more clinically ill than the others, there is a 30% mortality. In a beta-blocker trial of over 2,000 American males, after controlling for all major risk factors those who reported being socially isolated and having 'high stress' in their life had a four times higher death rate in the first year than the others.[4] A study in the USA that monitored patients' psychological status by a short telephone questionnaire given monthly, and intervened with support if they showed evidence of being 'stressed', reduced mortality by 50% in the year immediately post-myocardial infarction.[5]

The findings on impairment and disability may be summarised as follows:

1. In the majority of patients with chronic coronary artery disease disability is only weakly related to the degree of impairment.
2. At least some of the missing variance appears to be related to psychological and behavioural variables (ie what the patient decided to *do* about his illness).
3. There may be a direct physiological interaction between the correlates of distress, ischaemia and early mortality.

The mind and outcome

How can psychological factors affect outcome? At the most obvious level the patient's mind plays a vital part through the decisions he makes. Coronary artery disease is a largely self-inflicted illness, and the post-myocardial infarction patient's decision to stop smoking, lose weight, take more exercise and spend more time with his family may be the most important factor in both medical and quality-of-life terms. Indeed, a year after myocardial infarction 20% of patients say that it has improved their quality of life. For this 20%, education and a severe fright have been enough to change their behaviour — unfortunately, for many patients, this is not the case. As much western disease is similarly self-inflicted, discovering how to help the population change its lifestyle might be regarded as one of the most important questions in medicine today. Although large sums are spent on education through campaigns in the mass media, surprisingly little effort or money is devoted to the scientific study of this question.

Psychological predictors of disability

For those in whom primary prevention is too late, a great deal of work has been done in the 20 years since the Turku conference called for psychologists and psychiatrists to become involved in cardiac rehabilitation. There is now a good idea of at least some of the predictors of disability which operate independently of impairment:

*   previous psychiatric morbidity;
*   the patient's attitude to illness — what Mayou has characterised as 'an overcautious passive attitude';
*   the family's psychological response and behaviour, especially anxiety and over-protectiveness;
*   the patient's perception of his health status;
*   the number of 'cardiac misconceptions' held by the patient;
*   the patient's beliefs about causes of coronary artery disease.

Anxiety, depression and, to a lesser extent, 'personality' have all been extensively discussed elsewhere, so this discussion will concentrate mainly on the less widely studied and understood aspects: the 'cognitive' aspects, the thoughts and beliefs, that predict disability.

Two health psychologists followed up 200 post-myocardial infarction patients for five years and measured a number of medical and psychological variables throughout this period.[6] Patients were asked to rate their 'global health': considering everything about themselves, how healthy they thought they were. Immediately post-infarction 67% of the patients categorised their global health as having been 'high' prior to the infarct. At discharge from hospital, only 20% rated their health as high, by six weeks this had risen to 30% but between six weeks and five years there was no further improvement. Global health was related to the quality of their psychosocial recovery, but *not* to the degree of impairment or to their self-rated functional ability. The majority of these patients knew that they could function as well as before their infarct, yet still rated themselves as sick people. What is the reason for this? Maeland and Harvik found that one of the strongest predictors of a patient continuing to rate himself as having a very low health status was the number of what they called 'cardiac misconceptions' the patient endorsed.[6]

Cardiac misconceptions and health beliefs

Typical cardiac misconceptions about myocardial infarction are that:

- someone who has had a heart attack will have further myocardial infarctions until one kills him;

- any sudden shock or excitement could kill a person who has a myocardial infarction;

- orgasm is dangerous for people who have had a heart attack;

- after a myocardial infarction there is a dead part of the heart that could burst if it is put under too much pressure (this one belief was the best predictor the authors could discover of return to hospital with negative findings in the first six months after discharge); and

- heart attacks are caused by worry, stress or overwork.

The last misconception is ubiquitous both in patients and in the lay community. A study by Fielding[7] is particularly interesting. His post-myocardial infarction patients had just been through a cardiac rehabilitation programme in which the medical model of heart disease had been explained to them. Despite this, 80% of the patients still gave worry, stress or overwork as the main cause of their heart attack. They also mentioned the 'official' risk factors that they had just been told about — high blood pressure and cholesterol, smoking, etc. — and regarded them as undesirable features but not the *main* cause of *their* heart attack. The psychosocial factors were rated as the most potent and, except smoking (which was seen as almost totally controllable), the least controllable causes of their heart attack. The model held by the patients is thus significantly different from that held by most cardiologists today — and remains so, even after education to the contrary.

In an early study set up by the Australian government, a psychiatrist investigated why so few people went back to work following an uncomplicated myocardial infarction.[8] He reported that in 38% of cases failure to return to work was due almost entirely to one or more cardiac misconceptions held by the patient: for example, 'half my heart is dead and the other half is dying'. In a further 22%, the cause appeared to stem from a particular interaction with a doctor. For example, if the doctor said to the patient that he would be all right if he was careful, an anxious patient would often interpret this as meaning that he must do as little as possible — or else he would die. If the doctor told the patient that he had been lucky this time, the latter would think that meant he would not survive a second one. On being told that the heart attack was only a warning, many patients would believe that the doctor was telling them that a huge one was on its way any day.

What can be done if patients are so liable to misunderstand everything the doctor says? When these beliefs were investigated in the course of developing a treatment programme for post-myocardial infarction patients it became obvious that many of the patients who regard stress or work as particularly cardiotoxic have a view of the heart as being rather like a battery or a petrol tank. They believe that people are born with enough fuel in this tank to get them through a normal life, but if they have too much worry, work or excitement — even too much enjoyable excitement — it is used up more quickly than was intended. Many patients believe that the heart attack is the first warning that they are down to the reserve level in the tank, that their heart is 'worn out' by work, stress or worry and is getting unreliable. When the doctor tells the patient that he will be all right if he is 'sensible', the patient often assumes that the doctor is agreeing with him, his family and his friends that he should take life more slowly in future and, as far as possible, avoid stress, worry or hard work if he wants to live a normal lifespan.

Treating cardiac misconceptions

It has been described above that telling patients about the medical risk factors does not significantly revise their own beliefs about the cause of their myocardial infarction. It is also known from other psychological research that contradicting or arguing with a person is often the best way to strengthen his or her prejudice. Our message has to be integrated into the patient's model, and the debate conducted from inside that arena, if misconceptions are to be converted into more accurate beliefs that will lead to the patient acting in such a way as to maximise the chance of a good psychosocial and medical outcome.

One approach is to go along with the lay beliefs, to say the heart *is* the power centre of the body and therefore a bit like a battery; it *is* true that people feel very weak after a heart attack and someone with an unfit heart will definitely not have much energy — *but* what may not have been realised up to now is that the heart is recharge-able. By giving up smoking and taking exercise, an individual can increase the reserves of fuel and develop a stronger and 'fresher' heart than he had before his heart attack.

It is important to note that we are not talking here about a few 'neurotic' patients — 80% of patients believe that stress or other psychological factors are the most potent and least resolvable cause of their medical problem. Whilst they believe this, they are likely to act in ways that will maximise their disability, for example, by avoid-ing activity or excitement. In some patients this will lead directly to increased levels of symptoms — breathlessness, tiredness, angina and increasing anxiety. The anxiety may also produce new and alarming symptoms such as nausea, light-headedness, chest tight-ness, etc. All this generally serves to reinforce the misconceptions that activity is dangerous, the heart is worn out — and so on. Because of these beliefs, the patient and his increasingly anxious family are likely to increase the amount of rest and withdrawal from the normal pleasures of life. To reduce disability such factors must be taken into consideration in the routine management of *all* cardiac patients.

In some quarters this is now becoming accepted. A recent review and statement of guidelines by the World Health Organisation[9] suggest that cardiac rehabilitation should begin from the moment of diagnosis or, in the case of myocardial infarction, as soon as the acute event is stabilised.

An integrated approach to rehabilitation

By the time of discharge from the coronary care unit, preferably to a step-down ward, patients and their families should have begun to have their cardiac misconceptions examined and altered in a favourable direction. This process should be continued throughout recuperation. They also obviously need the more usual form of education about secondary prevention, which should be delivered in line with what is known about changing health behaviours. Failing this, at least advice should be consistent. Great uncertainty and distress are caused by the conflicting medical information and advice many patients receive from different sources.

Prior to discharge from hospital, patients and their families need a clear *method* and plan of action for *systematically* returning to previous activity levels, and to have discussed a detailed plan of how to get back to (the best aspects) of their 'old selves'. A simple home-based exercise programme can be helpful in quickly restoring fitness lost in hospital, and in shaping up to a new and less sedentary lifestyle whilst the motivation to change is still high.

Patients also need to be educated about the 'normal' psychological sequelae of traumatic events: poor concentration and memory, sleep loss, irritability, the symptoms of anxiety such as palpitations, nausea and panic. 'Home-coming depression' is almost universal in patients. If the patients are not warned about this, they commonly attribute it to their mind being 'damaged during the heart attack'. Cardiac misconceptions are endemic in society, and patients and their families need to be helped to be able to deal effectively with friends and neighbours and their cautionary tales.

What evidence is there that integrating this psychological therapy with routine medical care can improve outcome? A randomised study by David Thompson,[10] at that time charge nurse in a busy CCU in Leicester, had most of the features described above. The intervention began within 24 hours of admission, and patients and spouses received a series of time-limited counselling/educational sessions. These were particularly aimed at eliciting cardiac misconceptions and converting them to more accurate beliefs. In addition, each patient was helped to plan exactly what he would do when he left hospital and prepared for the possibility of an unpleasant psychological reaction. The intervention had a profound impact. Not only were a number of psychosocial problems reduced (eg anxiety and depression were reduced by nearly 50%) but these patients were also more likely to exercise in the desired way, to have given up smoking and to report a higher quality of life.

Self-help rehabilitation programme

If psychological treatments are to be integrated with routine care, they must be easy to implement and not demand large amounts of scarce resources such as time, specialist staff or space. With money from the Scottish Office and the British Heart Foundation (BHF) we spent four years developing a six-week home-based self-help treatment programme for myocardial infarction patients and their families. They are introduced to the material by a specially trained health care worker (the facilitator) before leaving hospital. The facilitator then contacts them three times by phone or a brief home visit (in either case limited to 10-15 minutes) whilst they are working through the material. This is in the form of six weekly written parts, a relaxation tape and a taped interview between a doctor and a patient in which the major cardiac misconceptions are discussed and the patient asks questions that many patients are too scared or embarrassed to ask.

A separate tape is given to the carer prior to the patient's discharge to deal with his or her misconceptions and worries, to encourage him or her to help the patient comply with the exercises in the heart manual, and to encourage the whole family to adopt secondary prevention measures.

The main components of the programme are:

1. The reduction/replacement of cardiac misconceptions.
2. Education about secondary prevention and the possible psychological sequelae of a myocardial infarction.
3. Mobilisation, starting with a simple, home-based, self-paced exercise programme, leading on to a daily walking programme.
4. Recording of activity levels in a diary over the first few weeks. This is checked by the facilitator at one, three and six weeks' post-discharge to provide encouragement, correct any misconceptions and increase compliance.
5. Self-monitoring through questionnaires and, when necessary,

referral to a separate section of written self-help advice on anxiety, depression, worries about sex, palpitations, etc.

6. Information on appropriate self-referral should the self-help approach prove inadequate.

7. Taped relaxation and written stress management programmes. Unless patients believe they have gained some control over stress they will continue to feel particularly vulnerable and may avoid returning to a normal lifestyle.

The heart manual was validated in a randomised, placebo-controlled trial.[11] The placebo was an equal weight of written material about what to do after a heart attack in the form of leaflets from various sources, including the BHF and other bodies, and an equal amount of facilitator contact. The results were remarkably similar to those of Thompson,[10] and showed a 50% reduction in cases of anxiety and depression. Patients who received the manual were significantly less likely to be re-admitted to hospital in the next six months and also visited their general practitioner less often (a mean of two less visits). Our contention is that this is at least in part because the patients' beliefs about heart disease have been changed, in particular about how likely they are to die prematurely. Patients were asked to rate their answer to the question 'how confident are you that you can make a good recovery?' on a simple 0-10 scale. At three days post-myocardial infarction there was no difference between the groups, but by six weeks (the end of the programme) the patients who had the manual were significantly more confident that they could make a good recovery. The confidence of the control group had not altered from baseline. Patients were also asked how they would rate their quality of life at six and 12 months on a scale of 0–10. Again, there was a highly significant difference between the two groups, with the manual group enjoying a significantly higher score.

Concluding remarks

There is an obvious role for psychological therapies in treating the relatively small number of patients with physical illness who also manifest psychological problems. However, it is the author's belief that psychology has a more fundamental role to play in medical treatment. Most physicians would agree that, in chronic illness, the patient's personality, how he reacts to the diagnosis and his subsequent behaviour can all be important modifiers of long-term outcome. Despite this, little is done in any systematic way to attempt to manipulate these variables. There is evidence, at least in coronary artery disease, that in many cases psychological and behavioural factors make a stronger contribution to disability than do physiological variables. The features that prevent a good outcome are often stereotypical within any particular illness. In some illnesses psychological and physiological variables may be relatively independent whereas in others they may work in a multiplicative fashion. To optimise treatment outcome, both medical and psychosocial, a greater understanding of these interactions needs to be developed, and then new ways of working with patients developed in which the psychological management is seamlessly integrated with the medical treatment. Until this is done, both in the patients and in those close to them, those powerful determinants of outcome — beliefs, attitudes, emotions and behaviour — will remain untapped or, worse, may be actively working *against* the best possible outcome.

References

1. Smith TW, Follick MJ, Korr KS. Anger, neuroticism, type-A behaviour and the experience of angina. *British Journal of Medical Psychology* 1984; **57**: 249–52
2. Williams RB, Harvey TH, McKinnis RA. Psychosocial and physical predictors of anginal pain relief with medical management. *Psychosomatic Medicine* 1986; **48**: 200–10
3. Medalie JH, Snyder M, Groen JJ, Neufeld HN, *et al.* Angina pectoris among 10,000 men; 5 year incidence and univariate analysis. *American Journal of Medicine* 1973; **55**: 583–93
4. Ruberman W, Weinblatt E, Goldberg JD, Chaudry BS. Psychosocial influences on mortality after myocardial infarction. *New England Journal of Medicine* 1984; **311**: 552–9
5. Frasure-Smith N, Prince R. Long-term follow-up of the ischaemic heart disease life stress monitoring program. *Psychosomatic Medicine* 1989; **51**: 485–513
6. Maeland JG, Harvik OE. Return to work after a myocardial infarction: the influence of background factors, work characteristics and illness severity. *Scandinavian Journal of Social Medicine* 1986; **14**: 183–95
7. Fielding R. Patients' beliefs regarding the causes of myocardial infarction: implications for information giving and compliance. *Patient Education and Counselling* 1987; **9**: 121–34
8. Wynn A. Unwarranted emotional distress in men with ischaemic heart disease. *Medical Journal of Australia* 1967; **2**: 847–51
9. World Health Organisation. *Cardiac rehabilitation and secondary prevention: long term care for patients with ischaemic heart disease.* Briefing letter, WHO Regional Office for Europe, Copenhagen, 1993
10. Thompson DR. A randomized and controlled trial of in-hospital nursing support for first time myocardial infarction patients and their

partners; effects on anxiety and depression. *Journal of Advanced Nursing* 1989; **14**: 291–7

11. Lewin B, Robertson IH, Cay EL, Irving JB, Campbell M. Effects of self-help with post-myocardial infarction rehabilitation on psychological adjustment and use of health services. *Lancet* 1992; **339**: 1036–40

7 | The place of psychotropic drug therapy

Eugene S Paykel
Professor of Psychiatry, University of Cambridge Clinical School, Addenbrooke's Hospital, Cambridge

This chapter will review the use of psychotropic drugs in medical patients. The antidepressants are the most important group of drugs in this context, but the other main classes of drugs, the neuroleptics and benzodiazepines, will also be considered briefly together with lithium. The main conclusion concerning psychotropic drugs in general is that they are valuable when used carefully and appropriately for their major psychiatric indications, but they must be used with caution outside these indications.

Neuroleptics

The neuroleptics (or major tranquillisers) have a limited place in the general hospital in confused patients. They are less liable to cause confusion than the other psychotropic drugs, and many geriatricians find small doses of these drugs useful in controlling confusion in the elderly. They should not be used for alcohol withdrawal since they are epileptogenic. They are also the principal group of psychotropic drugs which can produce irreversible side-effects: specifically the longer-term effect of tardive dyskinesia which is very difficult to ameliorate. The elderly seem more prone to this complication, which can develop after relatively short use such as a year or two. It is all too easy to leave a patient on the drug for a long period of time by default, and it is important not to do so unless essential.

Benzodiazepines

The benzodiazepines have been widely used in general hospitals for sedation and for relief of anxiety, but have fallen considerably in usage in the past decade. In fact, they may be quite useful in the short term. The problems result from long-term use; if they are used, there is a responsibility on the prescriber to supervise their cessation.

Lithium

Lithium has for some time been in common use in psychiatry. Most general practitioners (GPs) now have several patients who are being maintained on lithium, for whose management they are responsible. It is becoming increasingly common to find lithium among the collection of drugs that patients bring with them to the general hospital. The main problem with lithium is toxicity. In general, it is best to err on the side of caution for the physically ill patient on lithium.

Antidepressants

In considering the antidepressants, four general issues may be summarised and then applied to medical patients both in general hospitals and in outpatient clinics:

- evidence for their efficacy;
- who responds to antidepressants?
- how to use these drugs; and
- choice of drug.

There are surprisingly few studies in medical patients, and it is necessary to examine controlled trial evidence about the place of these drugs from parallel situations in more general psychiatric use. (Much of this evidence is reviewed in detail elsewhere.[1])

Efficacy

The efficacy evidence is extensive. A useful review of comparative trials of *tricyclic antidepressants* against placebo was published in 1974.[2] With the limited selection of six drugs then available in the USA (there were many more in this country), 93 trials were found. These were not unevaluated drugs but had been evaluated painstakingly. Of these, 61 trials (almost exactly two-thirds) showed the drugs to be superior to placebo, and 32 (one-third) did not. Many more studies would be available today and on a wider selection of tricyclic antidepressants.

What is the reason for the negative studies? There are always liable to be problems with methodology in drug trials. Some of these negative findings were due to low doses, short treatment periods or insensitive rating scales, but the major problem has to do with the extent of efficacy of antidepressants. In the individual studies, as a general rule, there are about 30% more good responders on the antidepressant than on placebo. The absolute levels vary with the study and with the kind of patient enrolled, but this 30% difference tends to be consistent. There are two reasons for this: first, antidepressants are of moderate but not overwhelming efficacy — some patients do not improve on them. This is particularly true of the most severe depressives who respond better to electroconvulsive therapy (ECT). Secondly, many subjects in trials improve on placebo, probably not because of the placebo itself but because of an amalgam of spontaneous remission and the effect of other non-specific interventions including admission to hospital and outpatient support.

There are similar findings with the other classes of antidepressant drugs. There is good evidence from placebo-controlled studies that the *serotonin reuptake inhibitors* are effective. In a meta-analysis of comparative trials against tricyclics by Song *et al*,[3] they were as effective as the tricyclics but no more effective. Indeed, no new antidepressant introduced on the market has been found to be more effective than the older tricyclic antidepressants, or conclusively more rapid in action. On the other hand, the Committee on the Safety of Medicines has high standards: no antidepressant introduced in this country in recent years has failed to be shown conclusively more effective than placebo, although efficacy could be questioned for some of the older atypical drugs.

There are fewer studies of the *monoamine oxidase inhibitors* (MAOIs), a minority group of drugs mainly used by psychiatrists. However, there is the same balance of about two-thirds of the older studies positive and one-third negative.[4] The new reversible competitive selective MAOI, moclobemide, has good efficacy evidence.[5]

Definitions of depression

Before discussing this issue, there is a need to be familiar with the concept of 'major depression' which has become prominent both in the depression literature and in official classifications in the last 10–15 years. It derives from an attempt to define a level of depression which it would generally be agreed is pathological and requires treatment. There appears to be a continuum of depression, from the perfectly normal mood that is universal, to the mood that is not normal but is understandable, to the disorder which at some point needs treatment. As the depression becomes more severe, it also becomes more pervasive and draws in more accompanying symptoms. It is particularly these accompanying symptoms that are the indicators of when the depression is pathological.

The definitions of major depression appear mainly in the American literature and vary slightly. The Research Diagnostic Criteria from the 1970s[6] require a period of depression of one week for probable, two weeks for definite major depression, four out of a list of eight accompanying symptoms for a probable and five for a definite major depression. (There are also some excluding criteria). These criteria also define a mild disorder, 'minor depression', requiring fewer accompanying symptoms from a longer list. In the more recent American DSM-IV,[7] major depression requires five out of nine symptoms for at least two weeks, of which one must be loss of interest or pleasure. The details matter less than the principles — the presence of a cluster of persistent symptoms going beyond simple depressed mood. The length of illness is usually much longer than two weeks in patients presenting for treatment.

Who responds to antidepressants?

Antidepressants are effective drugs overall, but which of the medical patients and patients presenting at the general hospital need them, who responds and who does not? To answer this question, it is not those patients who show the *most* improvement who need to be examined — since this might reflect a good spontaneous prognosis — but those who show the *greatest benefit* from active drug in terms of difference between drug and placebo.

Antidepressants in general practice

The best studied situation to answer questions about response is general practice, which is also the closest to the circumstances in the general hospital. There is a range of patients, the severity of depression tends to be less than that which the psychiatrist treats, and the same kind of issues arise of intertwining of depression with medical illness, so that the doctor needs to consider the extent to which the depression ought to be regarded as a normal and understandable reaction rather than as a pathological disorder requiring treatment.

A controlled trial was carried out in general practice of amitripty-line, a standard older antidepressant, versus placebo for six weeks, with a mean dose of 125 mg daily.[8] Two-thirds of the subjects satisfied the criteria for probable or definite major depression, and one-third for minor depression. Mean severity scores were relatively low. The drug was clearly superior to placebo, and a detailed examination showed that it was the core symptoms of depression which were affected.

In an extensive set of analyses the sample was broken down on various criteria such as demographic variables, previous history, severity and many different ways of looking at the understand-ability of the depression, the degree to which it was or was not pre-cipitated by stress and/or showed endogenous symptoms. In fact, it was only severity of depression that distinguished those who did or did not benefit from drug therapy; otherwise, in all groups, the antidepressant was of benefit. In probable and definite major depressives on the Research Diagnostic Criteria, amitriptyline was clearly superior to placebo; in minor depressives, although both groups improved, the drug group showed no greater improvement than the placebo group. In a more complex analysis in which the patients were divided into three groups on a severity scale for depression, only those in the most mildly ill group failed to show drug superior to placebo. (There are similar findings from an American study.)

The conclusion from this study is that the drugs are effective in milder depression but not in the *very* mild. It seems that only the severity of the depression is relevant in deciding whether or not a patient will benefit from the antidepressant. The threshold at which the drugs are of benefit for the patient presenting to the physician is below the usual definition for major depression. It is at the level where there is more than depressed mood — where there are a number of depressive symptoms, but not necessarily anything approaching a 'full house'. It is important to note that an under-standing of the depression in terms of precipitant stress did not dis-criminate response. Antidepressants should not be withheld in a persistent and pervasive depression simply because there is a precipitant stress and the depression is to some extent understand-able.[9] The stress is, however, an indication for combining antidepressant with support, counselling and psychosocial help.

How to use antidepressants

The two most important issues about clinical use of antidepres-sants are *dose* and *duration* of treatment. For dose, again general practice provides a good parallel. Psychiatrists have argued for higher doses, while GPs in the past have tended to use lower doses (this may have changed in recent years). In fact, the literature from controlled trials against placebo in general practice, although sparse, shows that low doses are not effective.[10]

There is a caveat. Certainly with the tricyclics, and probably the other antidepressants, there is quite striking individual variability at the extremes in the blood levels achieved by standard doses. For most people, the variability is not marked, but some people are clearly very sensitive and need less than the standard dose and have higher blood levels, while a few need very high doses to achieve the standard blood level range. This is important in medical patients, where severity of side-effects may render adequate doses difficult to administer and where there may be pharmacokinetic changes due to medical illness, interacting drugs or old age.

The second issue about the clinical use of antidepressants is that there are quite high relapse rates when antidepressants are stopped early, shortly after response, instead of being continued for several months. This has been shown in many double-blind studies comparing early withdrawal versus continuation.[11] Treatment should usually be continued for six months or until four months after complete symptom remission without residual symptoms, and then withdrawn slowly over about two months.

Choice of antidepressant

There is no lack of choice of antidepressants in Britain. Currently, there are on the market 12 tricyclics, four serotonin reuptake inhibitors, three other non-tricyclic uptake inhibitors, three atypical antidepressants and four MAOIs. What is to guide choice? Efficacy does not differ among the available drugs, except for doubts about a few rarely used older ones that were never well evaluated.

There is a copious literature on whether different types of patients respond to different types of antidepressant. Clinically, the differences are small. Tricyclics or serotonin reuptake inhibitors are the first drugs used in most situations. The debate as to *which* is not currently resolved, and concerns efficacy, costs and side-effects. At present, about equal numbers of psychiatrists and GPs favour starting with either a tricyclic or a serotonin reuptake inhibitor. My practice is to use a tricyclic as the first choice (as a better known, better evaluated drug which is much cheaper), and to save the newer drug for the special situations — which arise commonly in medical patients and will be detailed later. ECT remains the best treatment for the most severe depression.[1]

Antidepressants in medical patients

These general conclusions may now be applied to the patient presenting at the general hospital with depression and modified in the light of the available evidence.

Efficacy

Unfortunately, the efficacy evidence is limited. There are not enough controlled trials of antidepressant against placebo in medically ill patients, partly because these are not easy studies to do, given the risks of side-effects and interactions.

A number of controlled trials have found antidepressants superior to placebo, including studies of nortriptyline in parkinsonism[12] and stroke,[13] mianserin in cancer patients,[14] trimipramine in mixed subjects,[15] and phenelzine in depression associated with pain.[16] The study of nortriptyline versus placebo in patients with stroke who satisfied the criteria for depression is particularly informative. The drug was effective and superior to placebo, but there was a high drop-out due to side-effects.

When to use antidepressants

There is insufficient literature to draw specific conclusions about which medical patients will respond to antidepressants. The usual rule for deciding whether or not to treat a depression with antidepressants is probably appropriate here: the severity of the disorder and, without being rigid about criteria, whether the level of symptoms is approaching major depression. Provided that a persistent depressive syndrome is present, understandability should not be a criterion for withholding antidepressants. This does not apply in acute short-term crisis situations, such as bereavement or receipt of very bad news where there is no evidence to suggest benefit from antidepressants, but pathological persistent bereavement reactions taking on a depressive picture probably do benefit.

There are some studies in the atypical presentations, the kind of masked presentations seen commonly in the medical outpatient clinic. Studies of patients with atypical pain and with fatigue syndrome would suggest that antidepressants are effective in these situations.

There is a problem in assessing the diagnosis of depression in medically ill patients in hospital, where there is so much overlap between the symptoms of depression and those of the physical disorder. It is useful to try to divide the depressive syndrome into:

- mood;
- negative thought content, including any suicidal feelings;
- somatic disturbances such as of sleep and appetite;
- disturbances of activity and function; and
- observed depressive appearance and behaviour.

In medically ill patients the disturbances of activity and function, and also the group of somatic symptoms which feature prominently in the formal diagnostic criteria, are of much less value because they are susceptible to other explanations. However, the disturbances of mood and of thought content such as guilt, pessimism about the future, thoughts of suicide, and the depressed appearance, particularly agitation rather than retardation, are not susceptible to this problem. There is therefore something outside the mood disturbance itself to assist judgement of the severity and pervasiveness of the depression.

Choice of antidepressant

Choice of antidepressant is important in medical patients. The tricyclics may be problematic because they can interact with many medical conditions and the drugs used to treat them,[17] but they have also been the best studied antidepressants. The literature on interactions of the non-tricyclics is less detailed and there are fewer studies, raising the possibility that in time more interactions will appear. There is often greater uncertainty regarding the newer drugs, although their pharmacological actions are usually more specific and less broad than those of the tricyclics which affect many different receptors. For most patients, tricyclics are probably still the best first choice.

Special situations

Table 1 sets out some recommendations for special situations.

Cardiac disease. The literature on the cardiac effects of tricyclics is extensive. The main problem in therapeutic dosage is impaired AV

Table 1. Safer drugs for special situations.

Situation	Recommended antidepressant
Cardiac disease	Serotonin reuptake inhibitors Tricyclic antidepressants usually safe in *therapeutic dose*
Epilepsy	Monoamine oxidase inhibitors (moclobemide)
Overdose	Serotonin reuptake inhibitors Lofepramine
Confusion in the elderly	Serotonin reuptake inhibitors

conduction. Although in overdose the cardiac effects can cause death, in therapeutic doses the tricyclics are often unproblematic in cardiac patients. However, there is good evidence that the serotonin reuptake inhibitors produce fewer cardiac problems and also less postural hypotension (often a problem with the tricyclics). This is a special situation in which the newer drug carries benefit over the old.

Epilepsy. The tricyclics have undoubted epileptogenic potential in predisposed subjects. The literature and the data sheet statements on the serotonin reuptake inhibitors are slightly vague. They have not really been adequately studied in this situation. The literature suggests that there are differences between the drugs, and that there is some risk of provoking fits, but that the risk is less than with the tricyclics. The only antidepressants that are clearly not epileptogenic are the older MAOIs. The newer MAO-A selective, rapidly reversible competitive inhibitor, moclobemide, may have some advantages here. If there are problems, it is easy to stop rapidly because the drug loses its effect within 24 hours. Unfortunately, the literature on whether or not it provokes fits is inconclusive.

Overdose. Most patients with depression are not greatly at risk of overdose, but where that risk is present the safer drugs to use are the serotonin reuptake inhibitors and, among the tricyclics, lofepramine, which appears to have an excellent safety record.

Elderly patients. Tricyclics have had a bad reputation in the elderly because of their anticholinergic effects, particularly in terms of producing confusion, which is mainly due to muscarinic receptor blockade. This again may be a situation in which the newer drugs are indicated, although psychogeriatricians in this country are at present divided whether this should be as first choice or in those patients who experience side-effects on the older drugs.

Antidepressant use in practice

Two studies from the same group in the USA have looked at what happens in practice when medical patients are given antidepressants. In one study,[18] in which 95 antidepressant courses were prescribed to medical patients by the psychiatric liaison service (presumably using psychiatrists' doses), 32% of the patients had to stop because of the side-effects, particularly delirium, urinary retention and nausea. The response rate was 40%, which is relatively low compared with psychiatric practice.

The second study[19] considered 216 courses given by non-psychiatrists. The main finding here was of low doses: an average daily dose of 50 mg in imipramine equivalents. There was no statement about the number of people who developed side-effects or had to terminate treatment, but it may be inferred that it was less than in the first study. These results encapsulate the problem in using antidepressants in medical patients: adequate doses produce considerable side-effects, and low doses are not effective. It is important also to remember that pharmacokinetics may be disturbed in the ill patient, and that blood levels may be higher than usual. This may be one of the relatively few situations in which it is practically advantageous to assay blood levels.

Conclusion

Overall, the general conclusion for the antidepressants is that when the depressive syndrome has developed and there is a persistent depression with a number of accompanying features, an antidepressant is likely to be of benefit, irrespective of the psychological issues involved. It is important that in addition there be time for adequate discussion and counselling regarding these issues, and provision of social help where appropriate. A patient is receiving a bad treatment for depression if the *only* treatment given is an antidepressant. Nevertheless, used appropriately, judiciously and combined with psychological help and support, the antidepressants are of value in the medical patient.

References

1. Paykel ES. Treatment of depression: the relevance of research for clinical practice. *British Journal of Psychiatry* 1989; **155:** 754–63
2. Morris JB, Beck AT. The efficacy of antidepressant drugs: a review of research (1958–1972). *Archives of General Psychiatry* 1974; **30:** 667–74
3. Song F, Freemantle N, Sheldon TA, House A, *et al.* Selective serotonin reuptake inhibitors: meta-analysis of efficacy and acceptability. *British Medical Journal* 1993: **306:** 683–7
4. Paykel ES. Monoamine oxidase inhibitors: when should they be used? In: Hawton K, Cowen P, eds. *Dilemmas and difficulties in the management of psychiatric patients.* Oxford: Oxford University Press, 1990: 17–30
5. Paykel ES. Clinical efficacy of reversible and selective MAOIs in major depression. *Acta Psychiatrica Scandinavica* (Suppl) (in press)
6. Spitzer RL, Endicott J, Robins E. Research Diagnostic Criteria: rationale and reliability. *Archives of General Psychiatry* 1978; **35:** 773–82
7. American Psychiatric Association. *Diagnostic and Statistical Manual of Mental Disorders,* DSM-IV. Washington, DC: APA, 1993
8. Paykel ES, Hollyman JA, Freeling P, Sedgwick PJ. Predictors of therapeutic benefit from amitriptyline in mild depression: a general practice, placebo-controlled trial. *Journal of Affective Disorders* 1988; **14:** 83–95
9. Paykel ES, Priest RG. Recognition and management of depression in general practice: consensus statement. *British Medical Journal* 1992; **305:** 1198–202
10. Thompson C, Thompson CM. The prescription of antidepressants in general practice: 1. A critical review. *Human Psychopharmacology* 1989; **4:** 91–102
11. Paykel ES. The place of antidepressants in long-term treatment. In: Montgomery S, Corn T, eds. *Psychopharmacology of depression.* Oxford: Oxford University Press, 1994: 218–34
12 Andersen J, Aabro E, Gulmann N, Hjelmsted A, Pedersen HE. Antidepressive treatment in Parkinson's disease: a controlled trial of the effect of nortriptyline in patients with Parkinson's disease treated with L-dopa. *Acta Neurologica Scandinavica* 1980; **62:** 210–9
13. Lipsey JR, Robinson RG, Parlson GD, Rao K, Price TR. Nortriptyline treatment of post-stroke depression: a double blind study. *Lancet* 1984; **i:** 297–300
14. Costa D, Mogos I, Toma T. Efficacy and safety of mianserin in the treatment of depression of women with cancer. *Acta Psychiatrica Scandinavica* 1985; **72:** 85–92
15. Rifkin A, Reardon G, Siris S, Karagji B, *et al.* Trimipramine in physical illness with depression. *Journal of Clinical Psychiatry* 1985; **46:** 4–8
16. Raft D, Davidson J, Mattox A, Mueller R, Wasik J. Double-blind evaluation of phenelzine, amitriptyline and placebo in depression associated with pain. In: Singer A, ed. *Monoamine oxidase: structure, function and altered functions.* New York: Academic Press, 1979: 505–16
17. Fava GA. Depression in medical settings. In: Paykel ES, ed. *Handbook of affective disorders,* 2nd edn. Edinburgh: Churchill Livingstone, 1992: 667–85.

18. Popkin MK, Callies AL, Mackenzie TB. The outcome of antidepressant use in the medically ill. *Archives of General Psychiatry* 1985; **42:** 1160–3
19. Callies AL, Popkin MK. Antidepressant treatment of medical-surgical inpatients by nonpsychiatric physicians. *Archives of General Psychiatry* 1987; **44:** 157–60

Part 3
Delivering psychiatric care in general hospitals

The first two parts of this book pose a challenge for those delivering clinical care in general hospitals. If psychiatric disorder is common and affects outcomes, and it is treatable, how can services be developed and delivered to provide that treatment?

In this section an answer is provided from the three perspectives of the physician, the liaison psychiatrist, and the hospital business manager. We are aware that other people would also have a view. Particularly from the clinical side, nursing and clinical psychology have an important part to play. Good psychological care can best be delivered by multidisciplinary teams; any medical bias in the following chapters is explained by the nature of the conference from which they came rather than from a lack of commitment to that belief.

By the same token, good services will be best planned and delivered by considering the provision and commissioning of psychiatric and non-psychiatric services in unison rather than independently.[1] These and other matters are the subject of a report by a joint working group of the Royal College of Physicians and the Royal College of Psychiatrists,[2] which we hope will be read by all those who have an interest in this area.

References

1. Benjamin S, House A, Jenkins P. *Liaison psychiatry. Defining needs and planning services.* London: Gaskell, 1994
2. Joint Royal College of Physicians/Royal College of Psychiatrists Report. *Psychological care of medical patients — recognition of need and service provision.* London: RCP/RCPsych, 1995

8 | The physician's role in psychological care

Christopher Mallinson
Consultant Physician in Medical Communication; formerly
Consultant Physician and Gastroenterologist and Clinical
Director of Medicine, Lewisham Hospital NHS Trust

The psychological care of patients is a major part of a physician's work. For more than trivial or brief self-limiting disease, psychological factors may affect the physical outcome as well as the psychosocial course of the illness. All clinicians have a responsibility to manage, so far as they can, the psychological and social factors as well as the physical aspects of their patients' illnesses.[1] This is what makes a medical scientist into a doctor. There is, rightly, grave concern in the health professions that an imbalance has developed in which biomedical considerations of care tend to outweigh the psychosocial ones.[2] One response has been a joint working party of the Royal Colleges of Physicians and Psychiatrists, established in 1992, which has prepared a draft report on psychological care in general hospitals to be published in 1995.[3] Another has been two conferences organised jointly by the Royal Colleges of Physicians and Psychiatrists.

Physicians encounter four principal types of psychological problem:

1. Unexplained medical symptoms.
2. Organic (cognitive) mental states secondary to physical disorders.
3. Other psychological symptoms and syndromes secondary to physical disorders.
4. Physical complications of psychiatric disorder: these include self harm, factitious disease, abuse of alcohol and drugs, and eating disorders.

The first category was the subject of the first joint conference of the Royal Colleges of Physicians and Psychiatrists held in 1992.[1] The second and third categories are the subject of this book. Cognitive disorders in older patients have been the subject of a previous joint college report.[4]

The scale of the problem

A high proportion of patients attending general hospitals with physical diseases have psychological problems, amounting to an enormous number of patients in total. Some of them have psychiatric illnesses which are familiar to conventional psychiatrists but many have syndromes or associations of physical and psychological problems which are more familiar to physicians and to the small number of specialist liaison psychiatrists. The majority of these problems are found in patients with serious disease which is life-threatening, or is associated with chronic loss or disability, or causes severe symptoms or requires unpleasant treatment. The first four chapters of this book record a remarkably consistent prevalence (30%) of psychiatric disorder in such groups. Patients with physical conditions secondary to psychiatric illness are also common in hospital practice: for example, alcohol-related disease occurs in approximately 20% of male inpatients in medical wards.

Recognition by physicians

All the contributors to the first part of this book emphasised the large number of missed psychiatric diagnoses among general hospital attenders. For example, one survey of house physicians on medical wards showed that approximately 50% of psychiatric disorder was not recognised. Even though many of the patients showed histories of psychological disorders, only one in ten of those recognised was referred for psychiatric opinion.[5] It is evident that physicians have particular difficulty in recognising psychiatric disorder in the presence of physical illness. In one study, Goldberg and Bridges found that general practitioners (GPs) were 90% accurate in diagnosing psychiatric disorder when no physical symptoms were present.[6] Their accuracy fell to 30% when physical symptoms were present in somatisers. The familiar charge that physical symptoms take priority and provide a distraction from psychological diagnosis is well supported by the evidence.

A further problem is that doctors often fail to respond to obvious clues about their patients' emotional state even when such clues might be routinely expected, for example in patients with cancer and other serious diseases. [3, 7–9] The detailed reasons for this problem are discussed by Maguire and Howell in Chapter 5. Two major underlying causes are the lack of postgraduate education for physicians and the separation of the two branches of the medical profession. Another cause is the scanty provision in acute general hospitals of specialist help from hard-pressed psychiatrists and psychologists who are much occupied now in community care. In these circumstances, psychological care often becomes an 'add-on' task performed by doctors without the confidence and expertise which sound training, competent help and expert supervision can provide, and which patients have a right to expect. There is, however, good evidence to suggest that diagnosis can be improved by simple modifications in practice.[10]

How do physicians manage the psychological care of their patients?

Most common physical conditions can be treated in a standard manner, which differs little from one hospital to another and is accepted by the whole medical staff. In contrast, the psychological care of patients by physicians is haphazard — a product of individual experience, knowledge and interest, with wide variation within and between hospitals.[5] For example, antidepressants are often used unsatisfactorily by physicians, with much variation in choice of drugs, doses and duration of treatment, not always according to the precepts set out by Paykel in Chapter 7. Anxiety is frequently deemed to be treatable by simple explanation, with all the consequences of failure mentioned above. It is left to individual physicians to build networks, or even rudimentary multi-disciplinary teams, if they have the interest or local expertise to call upon. The evidence from this book is that diagnosis and treatment can be greatly improved with some modifications of current management, together with the use of well trained and supervised non-medical personnel.

Can physicians improve their diagnostic and therapeutic performance?

Clinical experience and the evidence cited both in this book and in its predecessor[1] leave little doubt that there is plenty of room for improvement. Given constraints of time, space, money and skilled mental health care professionals, what can be done?

Diagnosis

Simple, quick methods of diagnosis are required which can be incorporated into a busy clinical routine. Clues can be picked up from the referral letter or in the consultation (Table 1) and followed up. Anxiety and depression can be diagnosed reliably and

Table 1. Eight common clues given by patients somatising their psychological problems.

1. Specific symptoms: fatigue, atypical chest pain, abdominal and back pain, headaches not associated with organic disease or disproportionate to physical findings.
2. Numerous symptoms.
3. Overt tension in non-verbal communication.
4. Crying.
5. Increasing symptoms inconsistent with physical state.
6. Undue sensitivity on examination.
7. Presence of an inappropriately demanding relative or companion.
8. Fat folder — fat by reason of failed investigations or treatment, failed follow-up and/or dysfunctional consultations.

rapidly by a simple sequence of questions (as shown in Table 2).[10] Routine psychological screening methods can be valuable, but only if the clinician is willing to ask further questions to establish the significance of self-report scores and to determine the need for further intervention. Screening of mood, cognitive state or any aspect of quality of life is of little value unless the clinician knows how to use the findings.

The aim should be to integrate physical investigation with the psychological care. Whatever physical investigation is needed

Table 2. A sequential scheme of questions for use as a brief mood scale.[10]

Anxiety	Depression
1. Have you felt keyed up and on edge?	1. Low energy?
2. Have you been worrying a lot?	2. Loss of interest?
3. Have you been irritable?	3. Loss of confidence in yourself?
4. Have you had difficulty relaxing?	4. Felt hopeless?
If 'yes' to any of the above, go on to:	
5. Have you been sleeping poorly?	5. Unable to concentrate?
6. Have you had headaches or tightness in head or neck?	6. Lost weight (poor appetite)?
7. Dizzy, trembling, sweating, diarrhoea, frequency, tingling? (automatic anxiety)	7. Early waking?
8. Been worried about your health?	8. Felt slowed up?
9. Difficulty falling asleep?	9. Felt worse in the mornings?

Add 1 point for each 'yes' answer.
Anxiety states usually score 5+; depression usually scores 3+.

should be planned and explained to the patient. This avoids the familiar accusation 'they couldn't find out what was wrong' which so often follows negative results. The possibility that the tests may be normal should be explained in advance, and the prospect of a psychological explanation introduced early by an agreed method such as the re-attribution model described by Goldberg *et al.*[11] This is also the time to correct common misapprehensions such as those described in Chapter 5.

Treatment

Treatment should consist of simple measures of giving information and reassurance, together with a willingness to listen to the patient and answer questions. It is frequently helpful to involve a relative. Didactic advice is often ineffective because patients may not understand and also because it may not meet their particular anxieties and needs.[8] A discussion which allows the patient and family to bring up what matters to *them* is likely to be much more effective — especially if conclusions are agreed and recorded in the notes and also passed on to the patient's GP.[9]

It is also reasonable for physicians to use some more specific interventions for anxiety, depression and behavioural problems. The opportunity for such treatments will vary with the clincial setting. Physicians who care for chronic patients need more expertise than those working in acute units.

Anxiety. Explanation, discussion of fears, and information about the illness and treatment may well be effective. The Joint Working Party on liaison psychiatry also recommends simple anxiety management techniques, and occasionally the addition of short-term benzodiazepines or low-dose major tranquillisers such as thioridazine when necessary.[3] In addition to explanation, reassurance, discussion and other basic techniques of good medicine, physicians and the multidisciplinary teams may be able to use a number of more specific interventions, such as diary keeping, anxiety management and graded practice.

Depression. The recognition of the syndrome of major depression should normally lead to consideration of drug therapy. Tricyclic antidepressants, as Paykel concludes in Chapter 7, are still the mainstay of treatment for depression. No advantage in prescribing the newer antidepressants has yet emerged. The addition of cognitive behavioural therapy, available only to a minority, appears to improve long-term results. The report mentioned above offers helpful guidance on the way in which the diagnosis of depression is introduced to the patient.[3] It also recommends that clear warnings should be given to every patient about side-effects and the delays in onset of treatment. Weinman has reviewed the advantages of giving such information in writing.[12]

Behavioural problems. Behavioural difficulties in inpatient or outpatient management and in the use of medical treatments can often be dealt with by taking a fuller history and understanding the patient's viewpoint. Awareness of his or her particular concerns may then lead to ways in which treatment can be modified, and agreed in a manner that is medically sensible and acceptable to the patient. Physicians may have too little time for more than basic psychological management. In these circumstances help may be available within their own team or it may be appropriate to refer care back to the GP or to ask for specialist help from a psychiatrist or psychologist.

In some specialist settings extra help may be valuable. Chapters 5 and 6 describe the value and cost-effectiveness of trained specialist nurses in the recognition of psychiatric illness. Chapter 5 reports experience of a cancer unit in which specialist psychiatric treatment by the medical staff working with specialist nurses has produced a threefold decrease in psychiatric morbidity. Chapter 6 provides evidence that treatment by a specialist nurse can make an important contribution to the physical as well as the psychological outcome after myocardial infarction.

Conclusion

The psychological care of patients is a large part of a physician's work. It cannot be delegated wholesale to psychiatrists, nor can it be assumed that GPs will take up the psychological cudgels for every patient between hospital visits. Rather, it is part of the responsibility of physicians and those who work with them to recognise psychological and behavioural problems.

References

1. Creed F, Mayou R, Hopkins A, eds. *Patients with medical symptoms unexplained by organic disease.* London: Royal College of Psychiatrists and the Royal College of Physicians of London, 1992
2. Engel GL. The need for a new medical model: a challenge for biomedicine. *Science* 1977; **196**: 129–36

3. *Psychological care of medical patients — recognition of need and service provision.* Joint Report of the Royal College of Physicians and the Royal College of Psychiatrists. London: RCP/RCPsych, 1995 (in preparation)

4. *Care of elderly people with mental illness: specialist services and medical training.* Joint Report of the Royal College of Physicians and the Royal College of Psychiatrists. London: RCP/RCPsych, 1989

5. Feldman EJ, Mayou RA, Smith EBO, *et al.* Psychiatric disorder in medical inpatients. *Quarterly Journal of Medicine* 1987; **63**: 405–12

6. Goldberg D, Bridges K. Somatic presentation of psychiatric illness in primary care settings. *Journal of Psychiatric Research* 1988; **32**: 137–44

7. Audit Commission. *What seems to be the matter?* National Health Service Report No. 12, 1993

8. Simpson M, Buckman R, Stewart M, Maguire P, *et al.* Doctor-patient communication: the Toronto consensus statement. *British Medical Journal* 1992; **303**: 1385-7

9. Report of the Working Party on Medical Communication of the Royal College of Physicians of London, 1994 (in preparation)

10. A short mood scale. In: Goldberg D, Benjamin S, Creed F, eds. *Psychiatry in medical practice.* London and New York: Routledge, 1990: Appendix, p.5

11. Goldberg D, Gask L, O'Dowd T. The treatment of somatisation; teaching techniques of reattribution. *Journal of Psychosomatic Research* 1989; **33**: 689-95

12. Weinman J. Providing information for patients: psychological considerations. *Journal of the Royal Society of Medicine,* 1990; **83**: 303-5

9 | The role of liaison psychiatry

Christopher M Bass
Consultant in Liaison Psychiatry, Department of Psychological Medicine (Barnes Unit), John Radcliffe Hospital, Oxford

Liaison psychiatry may be defined as that area of psychiatry which is concerned with the diagnosis, treatment, study and prevention of psychiatric morbidity in the physically ill, of somatoform and factitious disorders, and of psychological factors affecting physical conditions. In a narrower sense, the term designates the realm of psychiatric consultation and collaboration (or 'liaison') with non-psychiatric physicians and other health workers in all types of medical care settings but especially in the general hospital.[1]

Psychological reactions to physical disease are common causes of referral to a liaison psychiatry service.[2] Feldman *et al.*[3] found affective disorder in 15% of medical inpatients, and that mood disorder was significantly associated with previous psychiatric history and social problems. Furthermore, 18% of men and 4% of women admitted to having a drink problem, and organic psychiatric disorder was detected in 31% of those over the age of 70 years.

Neither psychiatrists nor planners have realised the importance of the general hospital as a pathway to specialist care. Gater *et al.*[4] recently reported that general hospital referrals accounted for one-third of all new psychiatric contacts in a Manchester health district. These findings suggest that improving general hospital psychiatric services is as necessary as improving community care.

Although many general hospital patients with physical disease have psychological problems which might benefit from additional well planned help, only a minority need specialist psychiatric assessment (Fig 1). Others are more appropriately helped by either the hospital clinical team or non-specialist nurses.

A dilemma for the liaison psychiatrist is to know how to deploy scarce resources to meet the need of general hospital patients. Shepherd *et al.*[6] discussed a similar dilemma in primary care 25 years ago and concluded:

> The cardinal requirement for improvement of the mental health services in this country is not a large expansion and proliferation of psychiatric agencies but rather a strengthening of the family doctor in the therapeutic role.

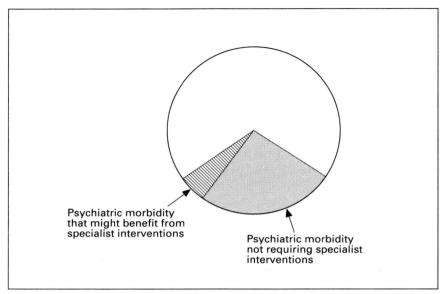

Fig 1. *The need for specialist intervention for psychiatric morbidity in the presence of physical disease.*[5]

Liaison psychiatry should have analogous aims: efficient consultation backed by liaison that aims to strengthen the therapeutic roles of the general hospital and primary care clinical teams in caring for general hospital patients.

Organisation of liaison psychiatry services

This chapter will describe how the psychiatric service can be organised in the general hospital by a multidisciplinary liaison psychiatry team. The demand is so great that the liaison psychiatry service cannot be expected to see all patients with psychiatric illness. An important aim, therefore, is to establish links with and educate non-psychiatric staff to identify and manage psychological problems. Before this can be achieved, however, it is important to educate hospital staff about the liaison service. In particular, information about resources, speed of response, indications for referral and 'how to refer' are important prerequisites.

Education of hospital staff

Education of non-psychiatric personnel is a key activity and should be undertaken in a systematic and enthusiastic fashion with as many hospital units as possible. Key units include the major medical specialties such as neurology, cardiology, gastroenterology and chest medicine, as well as oncology and transplantation. Educational activities should take place at different levels in the general hospital.

Doctors and general nurses

It is important that both doctors and nurses receive simple practical training in the recognition and management of common psychiatric syndromes. The standards of psychosocial patient care on medical and surgical wards can be raised by liaison nurses who can help heighten the other nurses' sensitivity to patients' psychological needs and increase their tolerance for disturbed or deviant behaviour. As a result, conflicts and crises related to unorthodox behaviour can be either avoided or better handled, and psychiatric complications either prevented or promptly identified and referred. Furthermore, the medical and surgical nurses can in turn influence the attitudes, practices and psychiatric referral habits of the house staff. It is important to note that it is often the nurses who initiate referrals through observations or complaints.

The basic skills that doctors and nurses need to acquire include the following:

- assessing organic brain syndromes;
- identifying depression and anxiety (if necessary with the use of brief rating scales);[7]
- managing disturbed behaviour;
- breaking bad news (to the patient and family); and
- taking an alcohol history.

One strategy for improving the skills of doctors and nurses is to persuade the medical and surgical specialty organisations to include psychological skills within their training and examination. The joint Royal College of Physicians/Royal College of Psychiatrists Working Group is striving towards this goal.[8]

Specialist nurses and other staff

Specialist non-psychiatric personnel in the general hospital, who take on responsibility for education and continuing care in many units, require both better training and more support to manage the psychological problems in their patients. Examples of such personnel include stoma therapists, renal dialysis nurses, breast screening counsellors, diabetes nurses, palliative care and human immunodeficiency virus (HIV) nurses. Unfortunately, specialist nurses are often appointed without any supervision or education built into their job contracts. This is unsatisfactory and regrettable, and these nurses will often seek support and guidance with difficult cases from the department of liaison psychiatry. It is also a cogent argument for having the liaison psychiatry service as a 'resource' for all specialist nurses who require advice or supervision of more difficult cases under their care.

Other staff who would benefit from being able to identify psychological problems include physiotherapists, midwives and medical social workers — who provide considerable psychological and social care, especially those who are attached to units such as intensive care and cardiac surgery. Social workers and liaison psychiatry units should have close working relationships so that they can co-ordinate their efforts and define their respective areas of expertise.[9]

There is enormous scope for improving the psychological skills of such personnel. An appropriate way of providing this is by supervision by either liaison nurses or psychologists. An example of the potential of such nurses was demonstrated in a recent collaborative study in Oxford with the cardiac department in which a cardiac nurse was trained in simple psychological techniques to counsel patients with chest pain and normal coronary arteries randomised to receive either psychological or usual treatment after angiography.[10]

Referral for specialist psychiatric care

Some referrals may require specialist psychiatric knowledge. These consultations often need integration of knowledge and contributions from several different disciplines for diagnosis and treatment, as outlined below.

Psychiatrists

Consultants cannot always be readily available for general ward consultation because of other demands on their time. However, links could and should be established for certain smaller units (eg neurology, gastroenterology and the pain clinic). Unfortunately, it is not infrequent for a particular consultant's opinion to be requested and this task to be delegated to a registrar. This practice is to be deplored for two reasons: first, it is bad professional manners and brings the department of psychological medicine into disrepute within the hospital. Secondly, it ignores the complexities of this borderland of medicine and psychiatry. Some of the diagnostic assessments in this area are among the most difficult and crucial in the whole of medicine. For example, it is not uncommon for the referring physician or surgeon to ask the psychiatrist the following questions:

- 'To what extent are this patient's symptoms attributable to organic disease?'
- 'Is this patient depressed or does he/she have an understandable reaction to disease?'
- 'Should I operate in this patient, for example, with a long history of recurrent abdominal pain but no evidence of mechanical obstruction?'

The outcome of these assessments may have both profound consequences for the future management of the patient and also economic implications if unnecessary investigations and hospital admissions are avoided. In the author's view, if a particular patient's problems are considered sufficiently complicated for a consultant's opinion to be requested, this should be provided. It is particularly important in patients with complex physical problems that co-exist with psychiatric morbidity, chronic pain and drug or alcohol misuse. A multidisciplinary pain clinic offers an ideal setting where patients with such problems can be assessed, often jointly with a pain clinic physician.[11]

Styles of response. The way in which the consultant psychiatrist responds to a request for his opinion depends very much on the nature of the problem and the situation (eg ward referral or outpatient referral). Three common types of response are encountered:

1. *Provision of advice,* with or without a prescription for a psychotropic drug, but the patient is not followed up. This type of intervention is not always successful, and may be associated with what has been called 'low concordance' — that is, the recommendations are not followed by the consultee.[12] The level of concordance is also associated with the timing of the consultation (it is lower the later it is held in the patient's admission), and with the experience of the psychiatrist (lower the more junior the psychiatrist).
2. *Consultation with systemic involvement,* involving physician, surgeon or general practitioner (GP), with the psychiatrist undertaking shared care with another hospital doctor.

Case 1

A 26 year-old nurse with multiple sclerosis was referred from the pain clinic where she was an inpatient. She was being withdrawn from pethidine, to which she had become addicted and had used to control chronic abdominal pain of uncertain cause. During her stay on this ward she had let off two fire alarms, having denied this initially. Her behavioural problems on the ward prompted the referral.

At interview she was in a wheelchair and dysarthric. Despite her disability, she spoke of returning to work and of 'being healthy like I used to be'. Her gross denial of the extent of her physical disability was striking, and accompanied by depressed mood, apathy and tearfulness.

In collaboration with the pain clinic physicians, the pethidine was tapered and she was discharged on amitriptyline — for both its antidepressant and analgesic effects. Her unrealistic expectations of the future were discussed with her husband, who revealed that she had taken many small 'overdoses' in previous years at times of life stress.

Several joint interviews with her husband were arranged to discuss the implications of her illness and ways of coping with the pain. Further meetings were organised with the rehabilitation centre, which she attended at regular intervals, and with the pain clinic, where she was seen jointly with the pain clinic physicians.

Major marital problems were dealt with in subsequent joint interviews, and further management was co-ordinated with the patient's GP, the social services, pain clinic and rehabilitation services. Over the next year she gradually came to accept the reality of her disease and her limitations, and worked harder and more willingly with her care workers to manage both her pain and her disability. In this intervention, the liaison psychiatrist was able to use both his knowledge of psychological reactions to physical disease and his established links with other specialist hospital departments to improve the quality of care of the patient.

3. *Major responsibility for the case,* where the psychiatrist consults the physician only infrequently if there are concerns about the physical disease.

Case 2

A 55 year-old woman was referred from a rectal surgeon, with constipation since the age of five. She had used and abused laxatives since the age of 11, and took 25–30 Senokot tablets each day to produce a bowel movement. Her referral was prompted by an inability to swallow her Senokot tablets although a barium swallow was normal. She had melanosis coli and had 'begged' the surgeon for a surgical solution (ileostomy) for her problem.

She had anorexia nervosa as a child and rarely attended school between the ages of 11 and 15. Despite this, she gained weight, went to university and became a teacher. At 28, her father died. This provoked further weight loss, but she continued to work until the age of 40 when she retired to 'write and draw'. She has never married and had an anxious and avoidant personality.

Over the course of six sessions, during which she was asked to keep a bowel chart, two important events occurred: first, the bowel chart revealed that she had approximately ten bowel movements every two weeks, which reassured her that her bowels were working. Secondly, it became clear that her 'swallowing difficulties' (globus sensation) started soon after her mother's death two years previously. She was able to make the link between the emotional response to her mother's death (of throat cancer) and the onset of her own difficulty swallowing. Once this link had become established, she realised that the 'constipation' was not as severe as she had originally believed. The Senokot was then prescribed in syrup form, and she became much less insistent on requesting an ileo-rectal anastomosis as a solution to her problems. She is now reviewed in outpatients at three-monthly intervals and no longer worries about her physical problems.

This psychological intervention was carried out in collaboration with the patient's GP. After full discussion with the surgeon (who was relieved not to operate), the liaison psychiatrist became the primary therapist and took responsibility for most of her care and support.

Psychologists

To run an effective liaison service the expertise of other professional groups is needed, particularly psychologists and social workers.

Psychologists are usually trained in techniques of psychological treatment and are best deployed either as supervisors of the clinical work of psychiatrists, liaison nurses and social workers or as therapists in their own right, taking on responsibility for a case load. They are not medically trained, and will often be asked to provide opinions on a different range of clinical problems from those of a psychiatrist — for example, in patients with exclusively functional syndromes. Psychologists should be integrated members of the liaison psychiatry team rather than members of a separate and unrelated behavioural medicine department.

Liaison nurses

A substantial body of research now demonstrates that psychosocial interventions in the medically ill not only improve medical and psychosocial outcomes but are also cost-effective.[13] Liaison nurses are trained in psychological treatment techniques and are an extremely important resource in the multidisciplinary liaison psychiatry team. There are many examples of fruitful attachments to units specialising in HIV/acquired immunodeficiency syndrome, oncology and plastic surgery/burns. The potential for further development is unlimited as an increasing number of hospitals become trusts with devolved budgets.

Need for liaison psychiatry beds

The provision of an inpatient unit to support a liaison service is a contentious issue. Some liaison psychiatry units have inpatient facilities whereas others do not. Most general hospitals of 500 or more beds require a designated number of liaison beds (perhaps between two and four), staffed by both medically and psychiatrically trained nurses. Such a resource is highly labour-intensive and costly, but possibly cost-effective in the long run.

In some general hospitals, if patients with physical illness become behaviourally disturbed and require specialist psychiatric nursing, extra nurses have to be 'purchased' from a nursing bank in order to 'special' the patient. This is paid for from the medical budget, and is unsatisfactory. Many clinical problems could be better managed in a liaison ward than in either a medical or a psychiatric ward: for example, patients with epilepsy and pseudoseizures; those with other neurological diseases such as stroke complicated by a psychiatric illness; patients with eating disorders; and those with co-existing physical and psychiatric disease where each is difficult to manage without addressing the other (eg severe asthma and panic attacks). The teaching potential of such an inpatient resource is enormous.

Conclusion

Psychiatric disorder is common among general hospital inpatients and outpatients. It is important to determine its natural history and to identify those areas in the general hospital in which psychiatric and behavioural problems are especially common. Many psychiatric and social problems are best managed by members of medical and surgical clinical teams. Liaison psychiatrists have a responsibility for organising and co-ordinating psychiatric services in the general hospital, including the education and training of medical and surgical staff. Another important activity is to inform purchasers of mental health care that improving general hospital psychiatry is as necessary as improving community care.[14] Further research demonstrating the benefits of liaison psychiatry interventions will help to achieve this goal, but liaison psychiatrists must also persuade their psychiatric and medical colleagues that psychological management should be a significant part of training, examinations and everyday work.

References

1. Lipowski ZJ. Liaison psychiatry, liaison nursing, and behavioural medicine. *Comprehensive Psychiatry* 1981; **22:** 554–61
2. Thomas CJ. Referrals to a British liaison psychiatry service. *Health Trends* 1983; **15:** 61–4
3. Feldman E, Mayou R, Hawton K, Ardern M, Smith EBO. Psychiatric disorder in medical in-patients. *Quarterly Journal of Medicine* 1987; **241:** 405–12
4. Gater R, Goldberg D. Pathways to psychiatric care in South Manchester. *British Journal of Psychiatry.* 1991; **159:** 90–6
5. Mayou R. *Consultation liaison psychiatry: an international perspective.* Upjohn International Inc., 1988
6. Shepherd M, Cooper B, Brown AC, Kalton GW. *Psychiatric illness in general practice.* London: Oxford University Press, 1966
7. Zigmond AS, Snaith RP. The hospital anxiety and depression scale. *Acta Psychiatrica Scandinavica* 1983; **67:** 361–70
8. *Psychological care of medical patients — recognition of need and service provision.* Joint Report of the Royal College of Physicians and the Royal College of Psychiatrists. London: RCP/RCPsych, 1995 (in preparation)
9. Hammer JS, Lyons JS, Bellina B, Strain JJ, Plaut EA. Toward the integration of psychosocial services in the general hospital. The human services department. *General Hospital Psychiatry* 1985; **7:** 189–94
10. Bass C, Mayou R. Chest pain and palpitations. In: Mayou R, Bass C, Sharpe M, eds. *The treatment of patients with functional somatic symptoms.* Oxford: Oxford University Press, 1995
11. Sullivan MD. Psychosomatic clinic or pain clinic. Which is more viable? *General Hospital Psychiatry* 1993; **15:** 375–80
12. Huyse FJ, Lyons JS, Strain JJ. Evaluating psychiatric consultations in the general hospital. *General Hospital Psychiatry* 1992; **14:** 363–9
13. Levenson JL. Psychosocial interventions in chronic medical illness. An overview of outcome research. *General Hospital Psychiatry* 1992; **14S:** 43S–9S
14. Mayou R. What should British consultation-liaison psychiatry be doing? *General Hospital Psychiatry* 1991; **13:** 261–6

10 | Setting up a liaison psychiatry service

1. A business manager's perspective

Susan Davies
Service Manager for Medicine,
The Lewisham Hospital NHS Trust

This section examines the process of setting up a liaison psychiatry service from a business manager's perspective. It considers the following issues from the perspective of different organisations:

- key steps in the process;
- potential benefits of a liaison psychiatry service;
- possible barriers to setting up a service; and
- possible sources of funding.

Establishing a liaison psychiatry service involves crossing organisational boundaries and it is essential to understand other people's views.

Key steps

The first step in outlining a service or business case is to identify the need for the service. This does not need to be a complex, scientifically argued and referenced process but should highlight the key indicators for providing the service. The second stage is to outline the service that it is intended to provide and to indicate how it will meet the identified needs. From this, it is possible to carry out the third stage which is to identify the cost of establishing the new service. This will vary according to the level of services that already exists locally. The most important points to bring out are the extra cost involved in setting up the service that has been described and also the cost savings (cost offset).

Once the costs are identified an essential parallel process is to promote support for the proposals. This depends upon the local situation and the relationships which exist either within the trust or between trusts and local purchasers. Most of us look towards the purchasers as a source of funding and it is important that they understand the aims and plans. Understanding how the

101

purchasers and other organisations might view the proposals is important as it may help either towards developing a more attractive case from their point of view or to talking through possible problems.

The final step before the service can be established is to identify and agree funding.

Potential benefits

It is usually helpful to outline the potential benefits of liaison psychiatry from the perspectives of the different agencies which might be involved in establishing the service. Not all these will initially believe that there is a realistic opportunity to provide a more appropriate form of care for patients with psychological problems, but the following might be considered:

Acute trusts

Access to a good liaison psychiatry service may mean more appropriate care and post-discharge follow-up for inpatients, and thus help to reduce length of stay. This will then release capacity either to allow other specific developments or to help a trust cope with its general workload. There is some evidence of such cost benefits of a liaison psychiatry service.

In the outpatient setting, more appropriate care could lead to a reduction in investigations, again either saving money or helping to reduce waiting times for investigations such as endoscopy. Earlier appropriate treatment or onward referral to other services might also reduce the need for follow-up appointments, thus meeting demands from purchasers that the number of follow-ups should be reduced.

Access to a liaison psychiatry service should lead to better trained staff. This should help to raise the reputation and profile of the hospital, particularly with general practitioners and the purchasers, which in turn should help to secure extra business.

Mental health trusts

A liaison psychiatry service in many mental health trusts will be a new area of work, thus leading to new investment and increased income. For a business manager, this is a 'good thing'. It may well be that the presence of a liaison psychiatry service will result in increased referrals to other services provided by the trust — again providing an opportunity to increase activity, and possibly income and reputation. It is also probable that, by improving colleagues' understanding of the general psychiatric services available, a liaison psychiatry service might lead to more appropriate referrals to current mental health services.

Purchasers

It is to be hoped that purchasers will be persuaded that a liaison psychiatry service can lead to a better quality of service, particularly satisfying the need to provide *appropriate* services. Reduced lengths of stay or waiting time for appointments will reduce costs for the purchasers and allow them to meet the waiting time standards set by the Department of Health.

Possible barriers

If these are some of the potential benefits, why will it not be possible to establish a hundred new liaison psychiatry services tomorrow?

The attitudes of individual clinicians

Some doctors will feel threatened by the prospect of establishing a liaison psychiatry service locally. Some, particularly those in investigational areas (perhaps performing excessive levels of investigation), might feel a threat to their specialty with the prospect of reduced activity. They may also feel that understanding a patient's psychological problem is not a part of their responsibility or interest and so may feel threatened by a liaison psychiatry strategy which promises to spread this responsibility to all clinicians. In these circumstances, it may be worth considering establishing a link locally between liaison psychiatry and a directorate in an acute hospital in which there is support from the clinicians. It will then be possible to establish a service which can prove its worth and be used to persuade other directorates to become involved.

Difficulties of achieving cross-organisational support

Establishing a liaison psychiatry service will involve crossing many boundaries, either between clinical directorates within one hospital or between mental health and acute hospitals, in addition to the need to secure the support of purchasers. We all work for organisations which have many competing demands and priorities. Trying to ensure that liaison psychiatry is seen as a priority service for up to three local organisations is a far harder task than developing a service within a single unit. This does not mean that it is by any means impossible, but it will involve much negotiation and care to achieve a continuing level of support from all concerned.

Funding

The third potential barrier to change is the need to identify new funding for the new service. An acute trust might be cautious about any suggestion that it should pay for the service provided by liaison psychiatry, and might also feel that the possibility of carrying out fewer investigations is a threat to its business. Equally, a mental health unit, requested by an acute unit to establish such a service, might feel unable to take on the full burden of providing this service. Purchasers might be cautious about paying more money for providing additional care to the same group of patients rather than to new patients.

Possible sources of funding

In view of the difficulties of funding, it is valuable to consider some possible sources of funding for a new service. These are by no means comprehensive but might be helpful starting points.

1. It may be possible to fund the development of liaison psychiatry from within current service resources and budgets. There is increasingly much more local influence in how money is spent, and clinical teams should be prepared to look critically at how they use their resources. Even if this does not release all the funding, purchasers may well be far more willing to talk to providers who are prepared to make some contribution or who have seriously examined the possibility of self-funding.
2. Although not a problem for London, some parts of the country are benefiting from growth money, and it may be possible to discuss with purchasers the possibility of using some of this to develop a new service.
3. There is increasing emphasis on the 'appropriateness of care' — care that is provided appropriately and not necessarily according to traditional patterns. Liaison psychiatry seems to meet this demand and it may be possible to bid either for

research and development money or for audit money to help establish this service. This is likely to take the form of pump-priming money for a one- or two-year period — but is no less useful for that.

4. A final suggestion is to consider 'sharing the risk' of this new development. If, in the process of establishing support for the service, it has been possible to gain in principle the backing of neighbouring units, it may also be possible to persuade them to contribute to the financial cost. Where there is a joint contribution to the cost of the service, the sums involved may be easier for the individual organisation to meet. I would also suggest that if each organisation contributes to the service, it will help to create a sense of ownership and commitment to that service, so enabling a successful liaison psychiatry service to be established.

2. A clinical director's perspective

Christopher Mallinson
*Consultant Physician in Medical Communication; formerly
Consultant Physician and Gastroenterologist and Clinical Director
of Medicine, Lewisham Hospital NHS Trust*

The changes of attitude, knowledge and skill which are needed to implement new practices in clinical practice are usually introduced by enthusiastic individuals willing to take on an extra personal burden of work. Such individual effort, while exemplary, cannot provide the integration of care across an entire hospital. In the same way, a single liaison psychiatrist cannot be expected to cope alone. Improved care needs the cooperative effort of several clinicians, good planning, budgeting and promotion within and outside the hospital unit. The hospital-wide policy needs to be carefully prepared and justified, and presented to all interested members of the clinical and management staff, the general practices, the health care systems in the community including mental health and, most important of all, the general public. Nevertheless, it will usually fall to one energetic clinician, usually the clinical director of medicine, to make the first enquiries and approaches and to come up with realistic proposals appropriate to the hospital, preferably related to the here and now, the art of the possible and the existing budgetary restraints.

In most general hospitals, the clinical director of medicine will be the appropriate clinician to work with the psychiatrist in setting up a new liaison psychiatry service. This section is an annotated outline of the process of creating changes in clinical practice, teaching and research.

Starting up the process

- A meeting with the chief executive, liaison psychiatrist, hospital medical and nursing directors.
  To define the needs, aims, methods and evaluation of liaison psychiatry in the trust.
  To form a steering group consisting of the liaison psychiatrist, a clinical director (usually medicine), a senior manager and a senior nurse.
- *Steering group*
  Take on the results of the above meeting.
  Summarise the existing strengths, weaknesses, opportunities and threats.
  Agree immediate activity, long-term strategy and provisional proposals.
  Arrange to put this information and suggestions to an open meeting and to individual clinical directorate meetings in order to brainstorm all concerned.

- *Open meeting*
  Invite:
  All interested health care professionals in the trust and in the local mental health unit, general practitioners (GPs), lay thera-pists, community health trust, community health council (CHC), patient support groups (eg MIND), patient focus groups (if any).

The meeting should begin with a brief statement of the present state of knowledge, concern, provision, shortfalls and practical suggestions for the future. Encouraging messages of commitment from the chief executive and medical director will help to persuade those present that the discussions can lead to real change. There can then be free discussion with the whole group or in several small groups to consider local needs and solutions. Project scribes should record carefully every suggestion without comment. At the end of the meeting there should be an attempt to list priorities, short, middle and long-term, and to agree ways of continuing the project, with tasks and timetables assigned to individuals, preferably with a known track record as achievers.

- *Clinical directorate meetings*
  Present proposals and discuss specific adaptations to the needs of each directorate.
  Discuss immediate course of action.
- *Evaluation meeting*
  Invite hospital audit officers, finance director, and members of directorates most likely to be affected by changes in practice, including radiology, pathology and clerical support services.
  Agree fruitful topics to be evaluated, aims, methods and timetable.
- Publicise the proposed changes in the hospital newspaper, Trust board and directorate documents. Fliers to all interested individuals and organisations in the community, including the local press.
- Improve the exchange of psychosocial information in communication, in particular between hospital and GPs. Consider a printed check-list on/or attached to referral letters each way.
- Brief check-list (digestible guidelines) on the diagnosis and treatment of common psychiatric disorders (eg anxiety, depression, alcohol, somatisation). Distribute to inpatient/outpatient staff, GPs, community health trusts, CHC and patient groups.
- Make known the existing psychiatric and psychological support facilities, whereabouts, waiting times and modes of referral.
- Publicise the changes in outpatient/inpatient management decided upon (and suggested below) and also the educational and research opportunities available.

Developing liaison services

Outpatients

The aim is to disseminate a uniformly high standard of care throughout the hospital. There are many patients to be managed — quite enough to justify regularly devoting one outpatient clinic in four or five to patients with demonstrable or suspected psychological problems. Such a clinic would produce a positive approach to psychological care and also provide an opportunity for building up multidisciplinary expertise. Experienced psychiatric nurses, clinical psychologists, social workers and lay therapists could all have a role. The clinic would also offer the opportunity for an interested psychiatrist, whether or not officially a liaison psychiatrist, to attend at least part of it to discuss particular cases at the end of the clinic with the whole team, and to introduce a consistency of approach, terminology, diagnostic methods and treatment. Such clinics could be of value in many medical specialties, gastroenterology, cardiology, neurology and respiratory medicine in particular — and indeed in surgical specialties such as gynaecology and orthopaedic surgery. The value of liaison psychiatrists and clinical psychologists in pain clinics is already well established, and is the subject of a recent report from the College of Health, *Living in agony.*[1]

In practice, this means making a regular commitment. It is important to keep the same location, and also nurses and medical staff who are familiar to the patients, but with additional help to avoid the pressures of time constraints.

- Encourage surgical and medical firms to have one clinic in four or five predominantly for patients with identified psychological needs. Provide additional psychological staff to work at them. Introduce training both in psychiatric diagnosis and in the use of psychological testing if needed. The liaison psychiatrist to come to at least part of each such clinic.
- Aim to create trust-wide knowledge, language, referral methods and clinical practice.
- Advance information for GPs and patients attending the clinic.
- Monitor results by audit and patient liaison.

Inpatients

- Introduce a scheme to search actively for psychiatric disease in the groups of inpatients known to be at high risk. If possible, establish teams of specialist nurses — equally important in surgical wards as in medical.
- Arrange the necessary treatment and follow-up system consequent upon the above. Adapt information, and possibly visit such a scheme in progress already (eg South Manchester).
- Make liaison psychiatry part of ward multidisciplinary team meetings.
- Ensure patient discharge letter has adequate psychosocial information (printed format?).

Education in psychosocial medicine

- Integrate psychosocial subjects into hospital postgraduate education by arrangement with all postgraduate tutors, nurse tutors and therapists. Senior managers to consider training non-medical staff in communication skills.
- Part of staff-round programme to involve liaison psychiatry team. Journal clubs include psychosocial subjects. Library material, including skill training, video tapes.
- Establish a network of teachers to give individual or small group training sessions in particular skills, examples of which are shown in Table 1.

This rudimentary programme will stretch the teaching capacity of the hospital staff. Recruit teachers from recently retired staff, Balint groups, GP trainers, psychiatric social workers, local university departments and patient support groups.

Table 1. Useful liaison psychiatry skills to teach multidisciplinary team personnel.

- Medical communication
- Self awareness
- Breaking bad news
- Dealing with difficult patients
- Responding to complaints
- How to examine the mental state
- Use of psychological screening instruments
- Reattribution methods
- Dealing with denial
- Detecting and converting misconceptions
- Using psychotropic medication
- Using psychological therapies

Research

Health service research is well funded, and behavioural scientific research is as respectable and indeed as rigorous as biomedical research. Explore possible projects with local university departments of psychology, sociology, social anthropology, etc.

- Monitor cost implications, knock-on effects on diagnostic and support services and bed occupancy.
- Use patient-liaison as a research opportunity.

Reference

1. Rigg M, Hogg C. *Living in agony; a patient-centred approach to chronic and recurrent pain.* Report of the College of Health, London, 1993